S

ECSTATIC CONFESSIONS

ECSTATIC CONFESSIONS

Collected and Introduced by

Martin Buber

Edited by Paul Mendes-Flohr
Translated by Esther Cameron

1817

Harper & Row, Publishers, San Francisco

Cambridge, Hagerstown, New York, Philadelphia
London, Mexico City, São Paulo, Singapore, Sydney

Originally published in German as *Ekstatische Konfessionen* (Eugen Diederichs Verlag, 1909).

ECSTATIC CONFESSIONS. English Translation. Copyright © 1985 by Harper & Row. Editor's Introduction Copyright © 1985 by Paul Mendes-Flohr. All rights reserved. Printed in the United States of America. No part of this book may be used or reproduced in any manner whatsoever without written permission except in the case of brief quotations embodied in critical articles and reviews. For information address Harper & Row, Publishers, Inc., 10 East 53rd Street, New York, NY 10022. Published simultaneously in Canada by Fitzhenry & Whiteside, Limited, Toronto.

FIRST EDITION

Library of Congress Cataloging in Publication Data

Ekstatische Konfessionen. English.
  Ecstatic confessions.

  Translation of: Ekstatische Konfessionen.
  Bibliography: p.
  1. Mysticism—Addresses, essays, lectures. 2. Ecstasy—Addresses, essays, lectures. I. Buber, Martin, 1878–1965. II. Mendes-Flohr, Paul R.
BL625.E3913 1985   291.4′2   84-48212
ISBN 0-06-061154-5

85 86 87 88 89 RRD 10 9 8 7 6 5 4 3 2 1

For Raphael and Ruth Buber

DAZ EINEZ ICH DA MEINE DAZ IST WORTELOS. EIN UND EIN VEREINET
DA LIUTHTET BLOZ IN BLOZ.

Meister Eckhart

WORDLESS IS THE ONE THING WHICH I HAVE IN MIND. ONE IN ONE
UNITED, BARE IN BARE DOTH SHINE.

Meister Eckhart

Contents

Editor's Introduction

In June 1907, Martin Buber (1878–1965) wrote the publisher Eugen Diederichs a letter informing him of "an anthology of ecstatic confessions" that he was then preparing. "The volume will present," Buber explained, "the utterances of fervent individuals from various ages and peoples that I have been collecting over many years. Aside from their great significance for the history of mysticism, they appear to be psychologically noteworthy, because they seek to communicate an immediate, wordless experience *(Erlebnis);* and they are aesthetically noteworthy, because of the strikingly unusual—truly unique—and wonderous poetic power with which they are expressed."[1]

In response to a query from Diederichs whether the volume would have a specific religious or confessional orientation, Buber replied that, although he intended including the mystical testimonies of many Catholics, especially of several little-known German women "such as the incomparable Benigna Königs," the projected volume would have as little to do with Catholicism as with Protestantism.[2] Further, Buber commented, the volume would be concerned "much more with the affirmation of life and a positive spirit than with asceticism and a flight from the world." It is, he added, "the communication of visionaries—individuals graced with dreams—about their innermost life." In conclusion, Buber noted that the volume had profound personal significance for him, and thus he would be most reluctant to entrust its publication to any publisher but one as spiritually and aesthetically sensitive as Diederichs. "I would gladly see this volume published by you," he wrote, "for as you know the quality of your editions pleases me. It also seems to me that this book, which should bring together entirely forgotten documents that are of utmost importance for the soul of humanity, belongs in your list of publications."[3]

The volume, *Ekstatische Konfessionen,* was accepted and published by Eugen Diederichs Verlag in 1909. Presenting voices of mystical rapture from various Occidental and Oriental traditions, theistic and pagan,[4] the volume was exquisitely produced.[5] Diederichs's exemplary attention to detail—the title page and calligraphic chapter headings were prepared by the renowned Jugenstil artist Emil Rudolf Weiss[6]—is indicative of the self-conscious aestheticism of the "new romanticism" of a generation that sought to overcome what was regarded to be the aesthetic and spiritual vapidity of bourgeois civilization—a civilization allegedly created by a mindless adulation of rationalism, science, and material progress. Decrying the "barren intellectualism" (as Diederichs once put it) of the bourgeoisie—and the attendant neglect of the unique, the beautiful, and the spiritual—this generation of pre–World War I central Europe cultivated an epistemological skepticism, finding redeeming value in aesthetic sensibility, profound "inner experience" *(Erlebnis),* and spiritual quest. And as Nietzsche once observed, "when skepticism mates with longing, mysticism is born."[7]

Mysticism (and concomitantly the suprarational world of myth) became the passionate interest of many, influencing the arts, literature, and philosophical discourse of the generation. A new trend toward mystical inwardness found expression in the poetry of Richard Dehmel, Stefan Georg and, above all, Rainer Maria Rilke; in the art of Wassily Kandinsky and "Der Blaue Reiter," and in the philosophical musings of Wilhelm Dilthey, Fritz Mauthner, and Georg Simmel.[8]

Flaubert anticipated the paradoxical mood of this generation when he exclaimed, "Je suis mystique et je ne crois à rien." ("I am a mystic and I believe in nothing").[9] Indeed, the interest in mysticism was not necessarily theistic, or even centered in God. Fritz Mauthner (1849–1923), whose critique of language, published in three hefty volumes between 1901–02,[10] made a singular contribution to the formulation of the philosophical issues of what was then celebrated as the New Mysticism, explicitly developed an atheistic, or what he called a "godless" mysticism.[11] A precursor of modern linguistic philosophy, Mauthner questioned whether language—intrinsically wedded to the *principium individuationis,* or the endless individuation and multiplicity of the world experienced through the senses—is a suitable tool for gaining and expressing genuine knowledge, especially of the world in its totality.[12] Gustav Landauer (1870–1919), a close friend of both Mauthner's and Buber's, succinctly summarized Mauthner's complex argument in his study of 1903, *Skepsis und Mystik:* "Language, the intellect, cannot serve to bring the world closer to us, to transform the world in us. As a speechless part of nature, however, man transforms himself into everything, because he is contiguous with everything. Here begins mysticism."[13]

The mystic's vision is beyond the world of individuation; it is beyond speech and thus incommunicable. The true mystic—Mauthner pointed to Meister Eckhart and Goethe—is aware of the fundamental ineffability of his experience *(Erlebnis),* which cannot be transformed into speech bound as it is to the *principium individuationis.* The ineffable beyond—an ineffable feeling of unity *beyond* the multiplicity of the world of ordinary sense experience *(die Erfarhrungswelt)*—can be felt or inwardly experienced *(erlebt)* but not properly articulated. "As soon as we really have something to say," Mauthner explained, "we are forced to be silent."[14] Yet, often the mystic, as Mauthner acknowledged, is torn between silence and a burning desire to communicate the content of his silence.

I shall attempt again to say the unsayable, to express with poor words what I have to give. . . . The world does not exist twice. There is no God apart from the world, nor a world apart from the God. This conviction has been called pantheism. . . . Why not? They are after all but words. In the highest mystical ecstacy the Ego [*das Ich*] experiences that it has become God. . . . Why not? Shall I quarrel about words? For a decade I have been teaching: The feeling of the Ego [*das Ichgefühl*] is a delusion. The unity of the individual is a delusion. If I am not me, yet exist, then I am entitled to believe that all other beings only appear to be individuals; they are not different from me; I am one with them; they and I are one. Are these mere philosophical word sequences? Games of language? No. What I can experience [*erleben*] is no longer mere language. What I can experience is real. And I can experience, for short hours, that I no longer know anything about the *principium individuationis,* that there ceases to be a difference between the world and myself. "That I became God." Why not?[15]

This conception of mysticism, particularly of "the difficulty of the mystic to grasp his experience in words, to express what he beholds, that which is not sayable," as Hans Dieter Zimmermann has recently noted, fascinated Mauthner's contemporaries.[16] Among them was Ludwig Wittgenstein, whose famous aphorism at the conclusion of his *Tractatus*—"What we cannot speak about we must pass over in silence"—echoes Mauthner's teachings.[17] *Mutatis mutandis,* Mauthner's language skepticism, is also Buber's point of departure in *Ecstatic Confessions.*[18]

Buber first encountered the then-fashionable monistic or pantheistic mysticism in the *Neue Gemeinschaft,* a circle founded by Heinrich and Julius Hart in 1900 in Berlin.[19] The central concern of the *Neue Gemeinschaft*—where, incidentally, Buber first befriended Landauer—was the problem of the *principium individuationis,* which the Hart brothers viewed as "the real motive force of all suffering and strife, all fear and doubt, all despair and misery."[20] The unity beyond the *principium individuationis,* "be it called God, Nirvana, absolute substance or bliss,"[21] they taught, is outside the "I"—the cognitive "I" that grasps the world in its multiplicity—but it is also essentially identical to it. In Heinrich Hart's words, "The world is a unity-within-multiplicity [*Vieleinheit*] and it is [thus] everything; nothing is beyond it; behind it is no thing-in-itself."[22] Unity is therefore not to be sought in a separate or *meta*physical realm. "Why do you seek the thing-in-itself and then declare it inscrutable, unfathomable? You are the thing-in-itself! You are God—the hub of the universe—the center of the sun—the core of matter—substance."[23]

Realizing that we ourselves, as part of the eternal flux of nature, are the thing-in-itself, we overcome the *principium individuationis,* the divisive world of individuated things, the world governed by space and time: "He who appreciates that he is the thing-in-itself and knows—unshakably knows this—has overcome time and space, and has become the universe, indeed eternity. His 'I' has become the great axis about which infinity spins."[24] Once the fundamental dialectical unity of the world is comprehended, the frightful abyss between the self and the world is bridged: "for one is always also the other. . . . The entire world is nothing but my 'I' and my 'I' is nothing but the world which is external to me."[25] As the "world-I" we partake in the eternal joy of becoming.

The mystical pantheism of the *Neue Gemeinschaft* had a profound effect on Buber's early conception of mysticism.[26] Thus we read in "Ectasy and Confession," his introduction to this volume: "What is experienced in ecstasy (if one may really speak of a 'what'), is the unity of the I. . . . [But] one cannot burden the general run of occurrences with this experience; one does not dare to lay it upon his own poor I, [for one] does not suspect that it carries the world-I; so one hangs it on God." Guided by this conception of the mystical experience, Buber became one of the most prolific students of mysticism and myth in pre–World War I Germany. After having completed his doctorate "On the History of the Problem of Individuation: Nicholas of Cusa and Jakob Böhme,"[27] which he submitted to the University of Vienna in 1904, he published in addition to *Ecstatic Confessions* a series of exceedingly well-received collections of mystical writings and mythic literature: *Die Geschichten des Rabbi Nachman* (The tales of Rabbi Nachman) (1906); *Die Legende des Baalschem* (The Legend of the Baal-Shem) (1908); *Reden und Gleichnisse des Tschuang-Tse* (The sayings and parables of Chung-tzu) (1910); *Chinesiche Geister—und Liebesgeshcichten* (Chinese ghost tales and love stories) (1911); *Kalewala: Das Nationalepos der Finnen* (Kalevala: The national epic of Finland) (1914); and *Die vier Zweige des Mabinogi: Ein keltisches Sagenbuch* (The four branches of Mabinogi: A Celtic book of legends) (1914).[28]

In these writings mysticism was conceived as an exceptional moment that takes the individual beyond the divisive world of individuation, a world which, of course, includes the social realm. Mysticism, as Buber then understood it, is thus a highly personal, indeed a decidedly asocial experience. In a debate with the sociologist Ernest Troeltsch, at the occasion of the First German Conference of Sociologists in October 1910, he rejected his colleague's reference to mysticism as a sociological category, insisting that the mystic's experience is properly understood as "religious solipsism":

I should like to pose the question whether mysticism can at all be considered a sociological category. I would contend that it is not: Mysticism is solely a psychological category. . . . Mysticism may likewise be designated religious solipsism. It is, on the other hand, an absolute realization of [individual] religiosity, achieving both an apprehension of one's self and an "apperception of God." In the intense exaltation of the self one establishes a relationship [*Verhältnis*] to the content of his soul [*Seeleninhalt*], which he perceives as God. On the other hand, mysticism seems to me to be rather different from religion, which is a sociological entity [*Ganze*] constituted by religiosity. It also seems to me that mysticism negates community—mysticism does not struggle with any organized community, nor does it set itself up as a countercommunity, as a sect would. Rather mysticism negates community, precisely because for it there is only one real relation [*Beziehung*], the relation to God. The process noted by Professor Troeltsch, the coming together of the believers, . . . does not at all occur in mysticism. The [mystic] remains thoroughly isolated in his belief [*Gläubigkeit*], for nothing else matters to him than to be alone with his God.[29]

Significantly, at the same time that he celebrated the ecstatic's triumph over the *principium individuationis,* Buber rejected mysticism qua flight from the world and its negation. In an essay of 1914, "With a Monist," he notes that in contrast to the mystic who annihilates the world—"in order, with new disembodied senses or a wholly supersensory power, to press forward to his God"—"I am enormously concerned with just this world, this precious fullness of all that I see, hear, taste." And Buber continues: "I cannot wish away any part of its reality. I can only wish that I might heighten this reality. . . . And the reality of the experienced world [*erlebte Welt*] is so much the more powerful the more powerfully I experience it [*ich sie erlebe*]."[30] But this affirmation of life, already expressed in the introduction to *Ecstatic Confessions,* was consistent with Buber's pantheistic mysticism and the search for unity *within,* or rather through, the concrete world.[31] Still the emphasis is on ecstasy, on an intense experience of what he was wont to call "an undivided unity" *(eine ungeteilte Einheit)*—and in light of these graced moments everyday life is at best viewed with ambivalence, either as a veritable obstacle or as a mere springboard to renewed ecstasy. "Over there now lay the accustomed existence with its affairs, but here [in the moments of 'religious experience'] illumination and ecstasy and rapture held, without time or sequence. Thus your own being encompassed a life here and life beyond, and there was no bond but the actual moment of the transition."[32]

With the development of his philosophy of dialogue—formally inaugurated with the publication of *I and Thou* in 1923, but which began to crystalize during the First World War—Buber largely abandoned his interest in mysticism.[33] His new understanding of man's relation to God led him to the conviction that authentic religious *devotio* must take place in the matrix of everyday life, in the realm of interpersonal relations. (It may be further noted that, in contrast to his earlier pantheistic mysticism, dialogue is grounded in a firm belief in a theistic, personal God whose active relation to man does not obscure the ontological or "primal" distance *(Urdistanz)* between the "I and Thou.")

To be sure, there are still traces of his youthful mysticism in his dialogical thought: The *principium individuationis* remains implicit in his epistemology; and the central categories of his mysticism—presence, presentness, immediacy, ineffability[34]—although now radically reinterpreted continue to inform Buber's philosophical reflections.[35] There is thus both biographical and philosophical interest in Buber's mystical writings, of which *Ecstatic Confessions* was undoubtedly his most ambitious project. This unique collection of mystical testimonies, which is regarded as one of the most enduring documents of German expressionism,[36] exercised a profound influence on Buber's contemporaries.[37]

No one perhaps read *Ecstatic Confessions* as carefully as the Austrian novelist Robert Musil (1880–1942), who kept a special copybook in which he transcribed numerous excerpts from Buber's collection.[38] These excerpts later served Musil in the composition of the many excurses on mysticism in his novel *The Man Without Qualities*—published in three volumes from 1930 to 1942, although it had its inception before the First World War. Containing close to three hundred citations from *Ecstatic Confessions,*[39] Musil's novel presents an understanding of these mystical testimonies—and their message for the modern reader—that subtly captures the spirit of Buber's volume.

The Man Without Qualities is a sustained meditation on what Musil's generation widely regarded as the collapse of bourgeois civilization, a process which for many was symbolized by the growing loss of confidence in language as a means for conceptualizing and communicating reality. Indeed, since the *fin de siècle* there was an ever-deepening feeling that language fails us, especially, as Musil would put it, to explain what is most real—our "innermost being"—to others.[40] This realization that language was inherently "faulty and fraudulent" bespoke not only the disintegration of culture but also the utter isolation of the individual, as Musil's contemporary and fellow Austrian writer Hugo von Hofmannsthal

(1874–1929) declared in his fictional letter—which haunted his generation—of Lord Chandos (1902):

> I have entirely lost the capacity to think or speak of anything at all coherently. At first it became more and more impossible to treat some sublime or general theme and in the process assume the sort of language that men are accustomed to use automatically. . . . [The] abstract terms one's tongue adopts as matter of course, in order to utter a sentence at all, now crumbled in my mouth like rotten toadstools. . . . Gradually the assault spread like a corrosive rust. All the sentences of plain, familiar conversation, the one recited easily, with somnambulistic assurance, now seemed to me so spurious that I had to cease taking part in any such discussions. . . . All crumbled into pieces, the pieces into still more pieces, and nothing would allow itself to be bound up in a concept anymore. Lone words floated about me; coalesced into eyes that stared at me and made me return their stares: they are whirlpools it makes me dizzy to look into, they spin perpetually, and through them one enters the void.[41]

Sharing Hofmannsthal's skepticism and bewilderment, the hero of Musil's volume, Ulrich, is a man without qualities, a man for whom the conventional qualities and values no longer seem authentic. With the eclipse of the word, all seems to Ulrich so tentative, fragile, and threatening: "Try to form a literal picture of being 'seized' by an idea," Ulrich explains to his sister, "the moment you experienced that corporeally you'd already be across the frontiers of the lunatic realm! But that's just the way every word needs to be taken, literally, otherwise it rots away into a lie. Yet one mustn't take any word literally, else the world turns into a madhouse!"[42] In response to such musings his sister concurs, remarking, "One possesses nothing in the world, one no longer holds anything fast, one's not held fast by anything."[43]

Yet Ulrich refuses to yield to despair and cynicism. He remains firmly committed to the efficacy of morality and reason—although he would be hard pressed to defend either. Ulrich, as one commentator puts it, is "a man of faith who merely happens not to believe in anything."[44] This faith is paradoxical: Before the void of a harrowing doubt Ulrich implicitly affirms the search for a life of meaning ultimately grounded in morality, the spirit, and the intellect. This search, which determines the thrust of the novel, perforce takes Ulrich beyond the "frontiers" of morality and reason; to cross the frontiers—or as Musil calls them, "borderlines"

—one must "tear the tissue of habit" and endeavor to overcome the bourgeois "mistrust" for anything but the "normal" or "ordinary" mode of experience.[45]

Indicatively, Musil entitled the copybook in which he made the excerpts from Buber's *Ecstatic Confessions*, "Borderline Experiences" *(Grenzerlebnisse)*.[46] But, he stressed, these experiences are no mere "flights of fancy"; they are eminently real—and as such they must be recognized by the spirit, morality, and reason. Indeed, they provide access to the metaphysical ground of all that is true. "For rationality and mysticism are the poles of the age," Musil wrote in his journal.[47] They thus complement one another.

Reason, Ulrich suggests, must be stretched, so to speak, beyond itself, allowing the mind, the intellect, to "experience" and behold a deeper, albeit ineffable, reality. As a contemplative exercise of the reasoning mind the mystical experience is universally available. Showing his sister his magnificent library of mystical writings (in effect a "hypostasis" of Buber's *Ecstatic Confessions*), Ulrich exclaims:

Here are Christian, Judaic, Indian, and Chinese testimonies. Between some of them there lie as much as a thousand years. And yet in all of them one recognizes the same pattern of inner movement, one that diverges from the normal but which is in itself integral. Almost the only way in which they differ from each other at all is just in whatever comes from being connected with theological constructions, as it were a doctrinal edifice that supplies them with a sheltering roof overhead. What it comes to, then, is that we can assume the existence of a characteristic second, extraordinary condition, a highly important condition that man is capable of entering into and which has deeper origins than the religions.[48]

One need be, Ulrich comments, neither a "saint" nor a believer in God "to experience something of this kind."[49] Thus Musil has Ulrich ironically declare, "I'm not religious. I'm surveying the road of holiness with the question whether it would stand up to one's travelling along in a motor-car."[50] Assuming a more serious vein, Ulrich explains there are moments when "one becomes oblivious of sight and hearing, and quite loses the power of speech. And yet it's precisely then, one feels, that one comes to oneself for a moment."[51] Upon elaborating these thoughts, Ulrich's sister interjects, "So you think . . . there may be something behind it?

More than mere 'freak of fancy' or whatever the phrase one might use to play it down?" Ulrich retorts, "I do indeed!"[52] He then proceeds to read a long passage from a mystical text, which in fact is a citation from *Ecstatic Confessions*.[53] Struggling with his incorrigible scholarly, circumspect disposition, Ulrich counsels himself—and the contemporary reader—how to read these mystical texts:

If you could read straight through all these descriptions that men and women of past centuries have left of their states of divine ecstasy, you'd find that there's truth and reality somewhere there in all the printed words.... They speak of an overflowing radiance. Of an infinite expanse, an infinite brilliance of light. Of a floating "unity" of all things and all spiritual faculties. Of a wonderful and ineffable uplifting of the heart. Of flashes of knowledge so swift that everything is simultaneous and like drops of fire falling into the world. And on the other hand they speak of a forgetting and no longer comprehending, of everything utterly sinking away. They speak of an immense peace, an utter detachment from all passion. Of growing mute. Of a vanishing of thought and intentions. Of a blindness in which they see clearly, of a clarity in which they are at once dead and supernaturally alive. They call it an undoing of the self, and at the same time they declare they live more fully than ever.[54]

Acknowledging the imploring caveats of reason and common sense, Ulrich then challengingly asks himself (and us), "Aren't these [ecstatic confessions], even though flickeringly veiled by the difficulty of expressing them at all, the same sensations one has even today when it chances that the heart—'ravenous and satiated,' as they say!—suddenly finds itself in those utopian regions that lie somewhere and nowhere between an infinite tenderness and an infinite loneliness?"

Disclosing a unique dimension of the mystical experience, Buber's collection of ecstatic testimonies is still animated with a spiritual vividness, due in no small measure to the charm of his translation, which sought to render into modern German not only the enthusiastic, often halting, words but also the inner rhythm and texture of the original. Buber listened to these texts with an inner ear, so to speak. To preserve his special hearing of these testimonies, Dr. Esther Cameron has deftly translated into English Buber's rendition, rather than turning to the original texts themselves. The reader I am sure will share my gratitude for her admirable achievement.

In light of Buber's lifelong involvement as an interpreter of Judaism, the contemporary reader is struck by the comparative paucity of Jewish mystical texts in this collection, illustrations from the Jewish experience being confined to several short selections from the Hasidic masters.[55] But given the fact that at the time Buber prepared *Ecstatic Confessions* the very existence of a genuine Jewish mystical tradition was widely doubted, the inclusion of even this limited representation from the Hebrew tradition should be appreciated. Indeed, Buber viewed it as one of his primary tasks to introduce the educated European to the spiritual reality of at least one Jewish mystical tradition, namely, that of Hasidism.[56] Perhaps Buber felt he fulfilled his charge on this score with his at the time already published volumes on *The Tales of Rabbi Nachman* (1906) and *The Legend of the Baal-Shem* (1908). Still there may be yet another more significant reason for the spare selection of Jewish materials in the present volume.

Despite its vastness and variety, Jewish mystical literature provides relatively few examples of "ecstatic confessions," and, moreover, the attendant problem of the ineffability of the unitive experience does not greatly preoccupy Jewish mystics. This is to be explained by a fascinating paradox. On the one hand, in contrast to Christian and other mystical traditions, Jewish mystics did not regard language as an *impedimentum* to the experience of God and "the upper worlds"; in fact, Hebrew as a supernal language spoken by God himself is regarded as being uniquely capable of articulating the infinite truths of Creation.[57] On the other hand, although Hebrew is a divine tongue graced with the power to grasp noumenal reality, it was by force of circumstances largely a sacred language and thus not the vernacular in which one's fantasy and most intimate experiences would be expressed. Hence Jewish mystics have left few records in Hebrew—virtually the sole language of their religious writings—of ecstatic experiences.[58] This situation, in turn, helps explain the historical irony that, whereas Jewish mystics who affirmed the noumenal power of language remained for the most part silent about their experience, confining themselves to theosophic reflections, Christian ecstatics—who, although assuming the basic ineffability of their experience, did not hesitate to record their religious feelings in the vernacular (and in the language of the church when it also served everyday life)— were rather expansive in describing the experience of divine ecstasy.[59]

Nonetheless, the genre of ecstatic confessions, however modest, does exist in Jewish tradition.[60] Of these testimonies that Buber might have also included in this volume, perhaps none is more fitting as a conclusion to this introduction than a passage from *Hovotha-Levavoit* (Duties of the Heart) by Bahya ibn Paquda of eleventh century Moorish Spain. Written originally in Arabic and translated into Hebrew already in 1161, this immensely popular pietistic treatise contains a vivid description of one who has made the mystical ascent to God's abode:

And that person will be in the highest of the degrees attained by the pious and in the most exalted rank of the righteous. He will see without eyes, hear without ears, speak without the tongue, experience things without the senses; appraise them without reasoning. He will not be impatient with any situation in his circumstances nor prefer any other lot than that which God has chosen for him. He will make his will dependent on God's will. . . . Of such a person the wise [Solomon] said: "Blessed is the man that heareth me, watching daily at my gates, waiting at the posts of my doors" [Proverbs 8:34]. It continues, "For whoso findeth me findeth life . . ." [Prov. 8:35].[61]

—Paul Mendes-Flohr
Jerusalem, May 1984

NOTES

1. Buber to Diederichs, 16 June 1907, Martin Buber, *Briefwechsel aus sieben Jahrzehnten*, ed. Grete Schaeder (Heidelberg: Verlag Lambert Schneider, 1972), 1:256. Years earlier Buber had submitted to Diederichs a proposal for an anthology of European mystical texts. See his letter to Gustav Landauer, 10 February 1903, *Briefwechsel aus sieben Jahrzehnten*, 1:186.
2. Selections from Benigna Königs, however, were not included in the published version of *Ecstatic Confessions*.
3. Buber to Diederichs, 20 June 1907, Schaeder, *Briefwechsel aus sieben Jahrzehnten*, 1:257.
4. Buber submitted the completed manuscript to Diederichs on 22 August 1907, appending the following note:

For the sake of the unity of the book I changed my mind with regard to the inclusion of nonpersonal pieces about ecstasy. Had I adhered to my original intention it would have resulted in a truly beautiful anthology bringing together Plotinus, Proclus, Stefan ben Sudaiii, Kabasilas, the Pseudodionysus, Bonaventura, Ruysbroeck, Nicholas of Cusa, Saint Bruno, John of the Cross *et cetera*. The volume, however, would have thereby swollen greatly, and at the same time obscured its basic character, namely, [a presentation of] personal *confessio*. On the other hand, I should like to include a personal testimony that does not speak of ecstasy, yet is thoroughly ecstatic: the essential part of Ignatius's Roman epistle (Buber to Diederichs, 20 August 1907, cited in *Eugen Diederichs: Selbstzeugnisse und Briefe bedeutende Zeitgenossen,* comp. Ulf Diederichs [Düsseldorf and Cologne: Eugen Diederichs Verlag, 1967], 168). Ultimately the selection from Ignatius, however, was also deleted.

5. First published by Eugen Diederichs Verlag of Jena in 1909, *Ekstatische Konfessionen* was issued in a revised edition by Insel Verlag of Leipzig in 1921 and reprinted in 1923. Aside from some minor additions, the revisions were confined to matters of style. Using unbound copies supplied by Insel Verlag, Schocken Verlag of Berlin reissued the volume in 1933 under its own imprint. (During the Nazi period, as an "Aryan" publishing house, Insel Verlag was obliged to transfer the rights of all "Semitic" works to a "Jewish" publisher, such as Schocken Verlag.) A facsimile of the original edition of 1909 was published in 1984 by Verlag Lambert Schneider of Heidelberg, with an afterword by Paul Mendes-Flohr. Buber's introduction to the volume, "Ekstatse und Bekenntnis" (Ecstacy and confession), was reprinted separately several times. See, e.g., Buber, *Die Rede, die Lehre und das Lied, Drei Beispiele* (Leipzig: Insel Verlag, 1917), and Hans Dieter Zimmermann, ed., *Rationalität und Mystik* (Frankfurt am Main: Insel Verlag, 1981). The present translation is based on the 2nd revised edition of 1921.

6. A friend of Buber's, Weiss also did the design and calligraphic work for Buber's *Die Geschichte des Rabbi Nachman* (Frankfurt am Main: Rütten & Loenig, 1906) and *Die Legende des Baalschem* (Frankfurt am Main: Rütten & Loenig, 1908).

7. F. W. Nietzsche, *Gesammelte Werke,* Edition Musarion (Munich: Musarion Verlag, 1920–29), 14:22.

8. On the modern interest in mysticism, see H. R. Müller-Schwerfe, "Neue Mystik," *Die Religion in Geschichte und Gegenwart,* 3rd ed. (Tübingen: J. C. B. Mohr, 1960), 4:1257–59; also see Grete Schaeder, *The Hebrew Humanism of Martin Buber,* trans. from the German by Noah J. Jacobs (Detroit: Wayne University Press, 1973), 54–106, *passim;* also see my "Fin de siècle Orientalism, the *Ostjude* and the Aesthetics of Jewish Self-Affirmation," in *Studies in Contemporary Jewish History, I* ed. J. Frankel (Bloomington: Indiana University Press, 1984), 96–139.

9. Cited in Schaeder, *The Hebrew Humanism of Martin Buber,* 90.

10. Fritz Mauthner, *Beiträge zu einer Kritik der Sprache,* 3 vols. (Stuttgart: J. G. Cotta'sche, 1901–02).

11. Cf. title of Mauthner's posthumous work, *Gottlose Mystik* (Godless mysticism) (Dresden: Reissner, 1925).

12. See Zimmermann, *Rationalität und Mystik,* 19–20. On Mauthner, see Joachim Kuhn, *Gescheiterte Sprachkritik: Fritz Mauthners Leben und Werk* (Berlin: W. de Gruyter, 1975), and Gershon Weiler, *Mauthner's Critique of Language* (Cam-

bridge: Cambridge University Press, 1970). On the general cultural context of Mauthner's critique, see Allan Janik and Stephen Toulmin, *Wittgenstein's Vienna* (New York: Simon and Schuster, 1973), especially chap. 5.

13. Gustav Landauer, *Skepsis und Mystik: Versuche im Anschluss an Mauthners Sprachkritik* (Skepticism and mysticism: Essays arising out of Mauthner's language criticism) (Berlin: E. Fleischel, 1903), 3. Landauer, who was to play a decisive role in Buber's life and intellectual development, edited Mauthner's *Beiträge* (see note 10, above); he also made the first modern translation of Meister Eckhart, *Meister Eckharts mystisiche Schriften* (Berlin: Karl Schnabel, 1903). On Landauer's relation to Mauthner, see Eugene Lunn, *Prophet of Community: The Romantic Socialism of Gustav Landauer* (Berkeley: University of California Press, 1973), 153–60.

14. Cited in Janik and Toulmin, *Wittgenstein's Vienna*, 131.

15. Mauthner, *Wörterbuch der Philosophie, Neue Beiträge zu einer Kritik der Sprache*, 2nd ed. (Munich and Leipzig: 1920), 2:131–32. Cited in Weiler, *Mauthner's Critique of Language*, 295. (I have slightly emended Weiler's translation and have likewise added some of the German in brackets.)

16. Zimmermann, *Rationalität und Mystik*, 16.

17. Ludwig Wittgenstein, *Tractatus Logico-Philosophicus*, trans. D. F. Pears and B. F. McGuinness, with an introduction by Bertrand Russell (Atlantic Highlands, New Jersey: Humanities Press, 1974), 74. Cf. "There are, indeed, things that cannot be put into words. They *make* themselves *manifest*. They are what is mystical" (Wittgenstein, *Tractatus*, 73). Wittgenstein's attitude to Mauthner, however, was ambivalent. See Janik and Toulmin, *Wittgenstein's Vienna*, 131–32, 196–97; and Weiler, *Mauthner's Critique of Language*, 298–306. On Wittgenstein and the mystical, see Auishai Margalit, "Wittgenstein's Pilgrim's Progress." in *Spiegel und Gleichnis. Festschrift für Jacob Taubes*, ed. N. W. Bolz and W. Hübener (Würzburg: Königshausen & Neumann, 1983), 233–38; and Eddy Zemach, "Wittgenstein's Philosophy of the Mystical," in *Essays on Wittgenstein's Tractatus*, ed. Irving M. Copi and Robert W. Beard (New York: The MacMillan Co., 1967, 359ff.

18. Buber knew Mauthner personally, having made his acquaintance through their mutual friend, Gustav Landauer. In 1907 Buber published a monograph by Mauthner, *Die Sprache* (Language), in a forty-volume series of "social-psychological" studies he then edited: *Die Gesellschaft* (Frankfurt am Main: Rütten & Loenig, 1906–12).

19. On the *Neue Gemeinschaft* and a lecture Buber delivered before the society, see " 'Alte und neue Gemeinschaft': An Unpublished Buber Manuscript," introduced and annotated by Paul Mendes-Flohr and Bernard Susser, *Association for Jewish Studies Review* 1 (1976): 41–56. Buber also lectured in the *Neue Gemeinschaft* on Jakob Böhme.

20. Heinrich and Julius Hart, "Unsere Gemeinschaft," in *Das Reich der Erfüllung*, ed. Heinrich and Julius Hart (Jena: Eugen Diederichs Verlag, 1900), part 1, 93. This conception of the problem of individuation was derived from Arthur Schopenhauer (1788–1860), who was rediscovered during the *fin de siècle* and who exercised a unique attraction for many thinkers of that period. On Schopenhauer's influence on Mauthner and Wittgenstein, see Bryan Magee, *The Philosophy of Schopenhauer* (Oxford: Clarendon Press, 1983), 286–315; also see Janik and Toulmin, *Wittgenstein's Vienna*, 206, 224, 244, 260. Landauer, it seems, introduced the *Neue Gemeinschaft* to Mauthner's critique of language as

a way of dealing with the problems posed by Schopenhauer. See Lunn, *Prophet of Community*, 144–65.

21. Heinrich and Julius Hart, "Vom höchsten Wissen," *Das Reich der Erfüllung*, Part 1, 16.

22. Heinrich and Julius Hart, "Die neue Gemeinschaft," *Das Reich der Erfüllung*, Part 2 (1901), 19.

23. Julius Hart, "Der neue Mensch," *Das Reich der Erfüllung*, no. 2 (1901), 24.

24. Ibid.

25. Julius Hart, "Von der Überwindung der Gegensätze," *Das Reich der Erfullüng*, no. 2 (1901), 40.

26. See Paul Mendes-Flohr, *Von der Mystik zum Dialog: Bubers geistige Entwicklung bis hin zu 'Ich und Du'* (Köningstein/Ts.: Jüdischer Verlag im Athenäum Verlag, 1978), 55–110.

27. For a copy of the dissertation, see the Martin Buber Archive. The Jewish National and University Library, Jerusalem, manuscript varia 320, folio 2/a. The dissertation is discussed in Maurice Friedman, *Martin Buber's Life and Work: The Early Years 1878–1923* (New York: E. P. Dutton, 1981), 79–81; and in Schaeder, *The Hebrew Humanism of Martin Buber*, 54–59.

28. Of these works the following have been translated into English: *The Tales of Rabbi Nachman*, trans. Maurice Friedman (New York: Horizon Press, 1956), also issued by Indiana University Press; *The Legend of the Baal-Shem*, trans. Maurice Friedman (New York: Harper & Row, 1955; Schocken Books, 1969). Several of Buber's most important essays on mysticism from this period have also appeared in English. See Buber, *Pointing the Way*, ed. and trans. Maurice Friedman (New York: Schocken Books, 1974), part 1. Also important for Buber's conception of mysticism, in particular for an understanding of his "transition" from pantheistic mysticism to a more existential, dialogical view of man and God, see Buber, *Daniel: Dialogues on Realization*, trans. Maurice Friedman (New York: McGraw-Hill, 1965).

29. *Verhandlungen des ersten deutschen Soziologentages von 19.–23. Oktober 1910* (Tübingen: Schriften der deutschen Gesellschaft für Soziologie, 1911), 206–7.

30. Buber, "With a Monist," *Pointing the Way*, 28.

31. Cf. Buber's letter to Maurice Friedman, 23 August 1953: "As far I understand mysticism, its essential trait is the belief in a [momentous] 'union' with the Divine or the absolute, a union not occurring after death but in the course of mortal life, i.e., as [an] interruption. If you read attentively the introduction to *Ekstatische Konfessionen*, you will see that even then, in my 'mystical' period, I did not believe in it, but only in a 'mystical' unification of the Self, identifying the depth of the individual self with the Self itself" (cited in Friedman, *Martin Buber's Life and Work: The Early Years*, 86).

32. Buber, *Between Man and Man*, trans. Ronald Gregor Smith, with an introduction by Maurice Friedman (New York: Macmillan Co., 1965), 13.

33. Buber's work on Hasidism, of course, continued unabated, but now his interpretation of this east European Jewish movement of "popular" mysticism was radically recast in light of his philosophy of dialogue. See Gershom Scholem, "Martin Buber's Interpretation of Hasidism," in *The Messianic Idea in Judaism and Other Essays on Jewish Spirituality*, ed. Gershom Scholem, trans. Michael A. Meyer et al. (New York: Schocken Books, 1971), 228–50. For Buber's critical evaluation of his own mysticism, see *Between Man and Man*, 13–14. With regard to his introduction to the present volume, "Ecstacy and Confession," it is

noteworthy that he decided not to include it in his book *Hinweise,* a collection of his essays from 1909 to 1953, stating in the foreword to this volume and with elliptical reference to "Ecstacy and Confession": "I have excluded— without any consideration of its philosophical or literary value—*one* essay whose basic point of view I could no longer stand behind" (*Hinweise: Gesammelte Essays, 1909–1953* [Zurich: Manesse, 1953], 6).

34. See Friedman, *Martin Buber's Life and Work: The Early Years,* 93.

35. For a comprehensive discussion of Buber's transition from mysticism to dialogue, see ibid., 93, 150–202; also see Hugo Bergman, "Martin Buber and Mysticism," in *The Philosophy of Martin Buber,* ed. P. A. Schilpp and Maurice Friedman (The Library of Living Philosophers, vol. XII) (La Salle, Illinois: Open Court, 1967), 297–308; also see Gershom Scholem, "Martin Buber's Conception of Judaism," in *On Jews and Judaism in Crisis: Selected Essays,* ed. W. Dannhauser (New York: Schocken Books, 1976), 126–197; also see Mendes-Flohr, *Von der Mystik zum Dialog,* 131–82.

36. See Georg Lukács, *Briefwechsel 1902–1917,* ed. Éva Karádi and Éva Fekete (Budapest: Corvina Kiado, 1982), 409.

37. See Zimmermann, *Rationalität und Mystik,* 25ff. For a synoptic review of the reception accorded *Ecstatic Confessions* by Buber's contemporaries, see Dietmar Goltschnigg, *Mystische Tradition im Roman Robert Musils: Martin Bubers 'Ekstatische Konfessionen' im 'Mann ohne Eigenschaften'* (Heidelberg: Lothar Stiehm Verlag, 1974), 33–34, 72ff.

38. Goltschnigg, *Mystische Tradition im Roman Robert Musils,* 63–71. A facsimile of Musil's copybook, containing 110 excerpts from *Ecstatic Confessions,* is presented in *Mystische Tradition,* 68–71. Musil made his excerpts from the 1921 edition of the volume. It should be noted that Musil's interest in mysticism preceded his reading of *Ecstatic Confessions;* cf. Robert Musil, *Tagebücher,* ed. Adolf Frisé (Hamburg: Rowolt, 1976), 2:1336 (an index of Musil's numerous references to mystical texts and works on mysticism going back to early 1900s). Also see Goltschnigg's comprehensive discussion of Musil's study of mysticism in *Mystische Tradition,* 53–62.

39. Goltschnigg, *Mystische Tradition,* 63ff.

40. Cited in Janik and Toulmin, *Wittgenstein's Vienna,* 118.

41. Translated by David Jacobson, in *The German Mind in the Nineteenth Century: A Literary and Historical Anthology,* ed. Hermann Glaser (New York: Continuum, 1981), 367–69. Cf. "Mauthner and Landauer corresponded with Hofmannsthal, whose *Letter* of the fictive Lord Chandos from 1902—yet another example of how language skepticism led to mysticism—could not have been written without Mauthner's influence" (Zimmermann, *Rationalität und Mystik,* 21).

42. Robert Musil, *The Man Without Qualities,* trans. Eithne Wilkins and Ernst Kaiser (London: Martin Secker & Warburg, 1960), 3:107.

43. Ibid., 124.

44. Eithne Wilkins, foreword to ibid., 14.

45. Musil, *The Man Without Qualities,* 3:117, 122.

46. Goltschnigg, *Mystische Tradition im Roman Robert Musils,* 68.

47. Cited in Zimmermann, *Rationalität und Mystik,* 12. Musil was wary of what he called "catchpenny mysticism" *(Schleudermystik),* the popular tendency to celebrate the irrational. Cf. "There are people nowadays who complain about intellect and try to persuade us that in their wisest moments they think by the aid of a special faculty that's superior to the faculty of thought. . . . [W]hat you

get at the bottom of the drained swamp is a bit of mushy rubbish!" (Musil, *The Man Without Qualities*, 3:128). The "light-of-day mysticism" *(tagheller Mystik)* that Musil seeks is neither irrational nor antirational; it is rather a form of knowledge, grounded in an awareness of the fundamental unity of the 'I' with the world, that *supplements* the individuating knowledge based on rational analysis. Cf. "I believe perhaps that some day before very long human beings will be—on the one hand very intelligent, on the other mystics. Perhaps our morality is even today splitting into these two components. I might call it mathematics and mysticism—practical amelioration and adventuring into the unknown" (Musil, *The Man Without Qualities*, 3:133).

48. Musil, *The Man Without Qualities*, 3:127.

49. Ibid., 122.

50. Ibid., 110.

51. Ibid.

52. Ibid., 111.

53. Cf. ibid. to *Ecstatic Confessions*, p. 129. See Goltschnigg, *Mystische Tradition im Roman Robert Musils*, 111.

54. Musil, *The Man Without Qualities*, 3:112f.

55. Nonetheless, some historians, assuming that Buber's interests were exclusively Jewish, refer to *Ecstatic Confessions* as "a collection of Jewish mystical texts" (Roy Pascal, *From Naturalism to Expressionism: German Literature and Society 1880–1918* [London: Weidenfeld and Nicolson, 1973], 171).

56. See the letter Buber sent to Eugen Diederichs accompanying a copy of *The Tales of Rabbi Nachman:* "You will perhaps recall that we once—several years ago—discussed the question of the existence of a Jewish mysticism. You refused to believe that there truly was such [a tradition]. With my Nachman book I have disclosed a series of documents from this [tradition]" (Buber to Diederichs, 21 January 1907, Schaeder, *Briefwechsel aus sieben Jahrzehnten*, 1:253f.).

57. I wish to thank my colleague Dr. Moshe Idel for elucidating for me this neglected subject of the Kabbalistic theory of language. For an innovative discussion of this theory, see his doctoral dissertation, "Abraham Abulafia's Works and Doctrine," submitted to the Senate of the Hebrew University of Jerusalem, 1976, vol. 1 (Hebrew with English abstract). Also see Gershom Scholem, *Major Trends in Jewish Mysticism* (New York: Schocken, 1946), 15, 17, 62, 134.

58. I am indebted to my colleague Dr. Ze'ev Gries for this insight. For a discussion of medieval Jewish attitudes toward Hebrew, see S. D. Goitein, "Some Comparative Notes on the History of Israel and the Arabs," *Zion: A Quarterly for Research in Jewish History*, n.s., 3 (1938): 104–10. Also see Ch. Rabin, "The Revival of the Hebrew Language," *Ariel*, no. 25 (Winter 1969): 25–34. In contradistinction to medieval Hebrew, and even when it was regarded as a sacred language, Latin often also served as a vernacular, everyday tongue for the educated Christian clergy, as was, for instance, the case of Saint Augustine. Gershom Scholem offers an alternative explanation of the Jewish mystics' reticence regarding "the supreme experience": "The Kabbalists . . . are no friends of mystical autobiography. They aim at describing the realm of Divinity and the other objects of contemplation in an impersonal way, by burning, as it were, the slips behind them. . . . It is as though they were hampered by a sense of shame. . . . I am inclined to believe that this dislike of a too personal indulgence in self-expression may have been caused by the fact among others

that the Jews retained a particularly vivid sense of the incongruity between mystical experience and that idea of God which stresses the aspect of Creator, King and Law-giver" (Scholem,. *Major Trends in Jewish Mysticism,* 15–16).

59. See Samuel Johnson's sarcastic comment about Jakob Böhme's garrulous "reveries" attributed to the fact that the German mystic achieved "the same state [as] St. Paul and to have seen unutterable things": "Were it even so," said Johnson, "Jakob would have resembled St. Paul still more, by not attempting to utter them" (*Boswell's Life of Johnson,* ed. George Birkbeck Hill, rev. and enlarged ed. by L. F. Powell [Oxford: The Claredon Press, 1934], 2:122f.). For an insightful discussion of the paradox presented by the prolixity of Christian mystical testimonies about the ineffable, see W. T. Stace, *Mysticism and Philosophy,* 2nd ed. (London: Macmillan, 1972), 277–306.

60. Cf. Louis Jacobs, *Jewish Mystical Testimonies* (New York: Schocken Books, 1975); also cf. André Neher, *The Exile of the Word. From the Silence of the Bible to the Silence of Auschwitz,* trans. from the French by David Maisel (Philadelphia: The Jewish Publication Society of America, 1981), *passim.*

61. Bahya ben Joseph ibn Paquda, *Duties of the Heart,* Hebrew by Jehuda ibn Tibbon, English by Moses Hyamson (New York: Bloch Publishing Company, 1945), 75. (I have emended Hyamson's translation some.) With respect to the present passage, it is perhaps not insignificant that Bahya was intimately familiar with Islamic mysticism. I wish to thank Professor R. J. Zwi Werblowsky for bringing this passage (as well as the comment by Samuel Johnson in note 59) to my attention.

Foreword

These communications by human beings concerning an experience which they felt to be beyond the human realm have not been collected for the sake of either a definition or an evaluation, but rather because in them the power of the experience, the will to utter the ineffable, and the *vox humana* have created a memorable unity. Whatever bore witness to these elements, whatever bore the marks of the Word, seemed to me worthy of inclusion.

I am not concerned with finding a conceptual "pigeonhole" for ecstasy. It is the unclassifiable aspect of ecstasy that interests me. Certainly it also has another aspect, by which it can be situated in the causal context of events; but that is not the subject of this book. The ecstatic individual may be explained in terms of psychology, physiology, pathology; what is important to us is that which remains beyond explanation: the individual's experience. We pay no heed here to those notions which are bent on establishing "order" even in the darkest corners; we are listening to a human being speak of the soul and of the soul's ineffable mystery.

It is something like freedom of the will. Of course, there cannot be any gaps in the great scheme of the cosmos *(Weltorientierung)*. Of course, everything is predetermined. But the human being has *felt free*. Refute this feeling with your notions! Prove that this feeling is an illusion, like the theologian's proving that God exists because everything has a cause and therefore the world too must have a cause. You laugh at the theologian: causality is valid only in the realm of outer experience *(Erfahrung)*. But perhaps inner experience *(Erlebnis)* is precisely what is beyond, because prior to, outer experience. I am the dark side of the moon; you know of my existence, but what you establish concerning the bright side is not valid for me. I am that remainder in the equation which does not come out even; you can put a sign on me, but you cannot dispel me. "You would pluck out the heart of my mystery?" This human being has felt free, has felt freedom, divine freedom, hovering above his actions. An illusion? Very well, then the illusion is for us the essential thing about him.

So it is with ecstasy: the word approaches us, the word of the I. I am including in this book the utterances of several individuals who are among those generally labeled mentally ill. Just as illusion is measured by the standard of "truth," so illness is measured by the standard of "health." But it does not interest me whether a doctor who examined Christin of Ebner would find her hysterical; what interests me is the way this female being speaks out of the urgency of her bliss. I do not know what madness is; but I know that I am here to listen to the voice of the human being.

Something aesthetic, then? No, not that either. I do not mean the words and whether they are beautifully put together; I mean the Word. This is another beauty than that of the aesthetic: the voice of the human being sounding in my ears.

The voice of the human being; and I have forgotten about degrees, the hierarchy of minds. There are the lofty Plotinus and Attar, the boldest of poets; there is Valentinus, the secret daimon of the turn of an era, and Ramakrishna, through whom the whole being of India was made manifest once more in our day; there is Symeon, the Byzantine friend and singer of God, and Gerlach Peters, his brother in the Netherlands, young and filled with the joy of dying; and there, beside them, are the shepherdess Alpais of Cudot (whose speech I find almost a bit too clever) and the wild farm-wench Armelle Nicolas; there are the Camisards, who make the right kind of confession for me, the confession of sin and salvation; there are those simple-hearted lovesick nuns; there are those ungainly burghers Hans Engelbrecht and Hemme Hayen stammering out their tale of wonder. There they are together, side by side, in the fellowship of those who dared to tell of that abyss. I live with them; I hear their voices, their voice: the voice of the human being.

As I have been seeking only this one thing, it will be understood why I have included here only a very small proportion of the vast material accumulated during my years of seeking. Why I have not included:

All nonsubjective discourse on ecstasy (though I have tried to distill the most personal element from certain apparently impersonal utterances, and have added in a supplement several significant documents of nonsubjective utterance from peoples and circles that could not be dealt with in the main part of this volume, together with an excerpt from the tract "Sister Katrei," which I did not want this volume to be without); therefore Philo and Proklos, Kabasilas and the Victorines, Ruysbroeck and John of the Cross are absent here;

all descriptions of visions of a nonsubjective character; that is, those in which the being of the beholder neither acts nor is acted upon (with the exception of one vision of Birgitta, which seems altogether subjective although she herself scarcely participates); thus I have had to leave out of consideration even such remarkable human beings as Joachim of Floris and Marguerite d'Oyngt, and especially such topographers of vision as Swedenborg, whose prodigious spiritual diaries have given me only a prodigious astonishment;

all that is said in scholastic or rhetorical, that is, indirect, fashion;

all autobiographical communications on ecstasy as an object of curiosity and analysis (here Cardano seems to me the most remarkable);

all poetic speech that proves to be a subjection of experience to rhythm, a replacement of what erupts and storms onward by a metrical rising and falling (among these I must count even Jacopone, one of my favorites); on the other hand, I felt that I could include here Attar, Rumi, Symeon, Mechtild von Magdeburg, and Seuse, a distinction which I can defend not by formulating a criterion, but only by referring the reader to the works themselves (in the case of Jacopone, this distinction was not easy for me to draw);

all treatments of ecstatic experience from a psychological point of view; that is, the sort of reportage that describes the experience as an event in the context of causality, objectifies it, issues not from the power of the experience as it continues to affect the speaker but from recapitulation and reflection, a contemplation as it were not of the after-image but of the image in memory; akin to this is the classifying depiction by the celebrated Teresa, and hence I have included only the most subjective passages from her work, and these not without reluctance.

On the other hand, I have excluded all that is fragmentary and has not developed into a form expressive of a personality; here, though regretfully, I have had to omit various passages from Indian and Gnostic mysticism, as well as some rich material from the Slavic sects (and indeed I have included, of all that I have gathered from the newer sects, only one representative Camisard confession; as to the older sects, only certain passages from the early Christian heretics seemed to me too expressive of essence to be left out).

Everywhere I have sought the immediate; yet I have not made immediacy of *transmission* a principle of selection. I have included confessions that were written down, not by the one who communicated them, but by others close to him (the words of Ramakrishna and others, in particular many documents of monastic ecstasy, are of this sort); occasionally the transcribers were somehow involved in the experience, as in that extraordinary testimony of a dual ecstasy recorded by Catherine of Siena's confessor; likewise certain anonymous things that withstood the examination (the "Song of Bareness" and that vision of the unknown "page"); even some things that are obviously legendary, in which the words of the ecstatic lived on, unmistakably preserved by the fidelity generations of believers bear toward the Word (for instance the early Sufis and Aegidius of Assisi).

I have not striven for completeness of any kind. Every basic type seemed to me adequately represented by a few significant passages. Only one domain has received more consideration than the book's symmetry warrants: that of monastic ecstasy. This is because I encountered here, beneath the external uniformity of a single institution, even a single regulation, a wondrously manifold life: here I could perceive most clearly how the human being's innermost experience is simultaneously the most personal and the most general, that by which the human being is wholly manifest as creature and at the same time as something unrepeatably individual. Thus in four centuries four Italian women succeed one another: in the time of Duccio and the last Byzantines, the contemplative Angela di Foligno, to whom all form is alien; in Giotto's time, the Sienese, fervent with all her body; at the height of the Renaissance, Catherine of Genoa, with her calm, clear self-certainty; in the Baroque era, Maddalena, whose stormy impetus carries her across all barriers. And, in an utterly small space and a very narrow time span: In the Töss cloister near Winterthur, probably in close proximity, lived two, Sofia von Klingnau and Jützi Schultheiss, of whom the first could experience only herself (but not something particular about herself, rather her entire I in everything), while the second could experience only the world (but not this, that, or the other thing in it, rather the whole world in everything); they experienced the same thing, and yet how differently! Many examples of the same kind can be found in monastic literature.

A second asymmetry disturbs me more: that I am presenting here much less from the Orient than from occidental Christianity. This is first of all because most Oriental languages are inaccessible to me, and of the Persian texts, for instance, very little has been translated into any European language. But there is something else: It seems to me that Asiatic literature contains relatively few real confessions. In the Orient, ecstasy is a far more frequent, ordinary, "normal" phenomenon than it is in Europe; thus it tends, instead of expressing itself in a particular confession, to flow into the works of the day: into a verse of love poetry, or an earthen vessel; one can read it off from a Persian couplet or a Chinese vase. Only rarely does the experience carve a particular channel for itself. Moreover, in the Oriental culture, unlike in the European, one does not hold up one's experience, as in lifted hands, to contemplate it as one's own; he feels: this is experienced.

This may suffice for an explanation of what is to be found in this book and what is absent from it. I must also say something about the way in which I have treated the texts. The intention of the book accounts for my having to cite excerpts, leaving out inessential passages (the omissions are always indicated by dots). I have translated the lyrical pieces into prose, since only in this way could I attain the degree of fidelity I needed. Only in a few cases have I made use of existing German translations. The editions and translations that I have used are indicated at the end.

I have not added biographies of those who have given us these confessions. The circumstances of their lives have nothing to do with what they communicate here. I have given only their time and sphere, in order to make it easier to place these often little-known figures along humanity's road.

—Martin Buber

Introduction by Martin Buber: Ecstasy and Confession

The commotion of our human life, which lets in everything, all the light and all the music, all the mad pranks of thought and all the variations of pain, the fullness of memory and the fullness of expectation, is closed only to *one* thing: unity. Every gaze is secretly crowded with a thousand blinking glances that do not want to be its siblings; every pure, beautiful astonishment is confused by a thousand memories; and even the quietest suffering is mixed with the hissing of a thousand questions. This commotion is sumptuous and stingy, it heaps up abundance and refuses encompassment; it builds a vortex of objects and a vortex of feelings, from whirl-wall to whirl-wall, things flying at each other and over each other, and lets us pass through, all the length of this way of ours, without unity. The commotion lets me have things and the ideas that go with them, only not unity of world or of I: it is all the same. I, the world, we—no, I the world am what is moved out of reach, what cannot be grasped, what cannot be experienced. I give the bundle a name and say "world" to it, but the name is not a unity that is experienced. I give the bundle a subject and say "I" to it, but the subject is not a unity that is experienced. Name and subject belong to the commotion, and mine is the hand that reaches out—into empty space.

But that is the divine meaning of human life: that the commotion is, after all, only the outside of an unknown Inward which is the most living thing of all; and that this Inward can withhold the experience of itself from knowledge, which is a daughter of the commotion, but not from the vibrant and self-liberating soul. The soul that has tensed itself utterly to burst through the commotion and escape from it is the soul that receives the grace of unity. Whether the soul meets a loved human being or a wild landscape of heaped-up stones—from this human being, this heap of stones,

grace catches fire, and the soul no longer experiences some particular around which a thousand other particulars are buzzing, not
the pressure of a hand or the look of the rocks; rather it experiences unity, the world: itself. All its powers come into play, all its
powers unified and felt as one, and there in the midst of the powers
lives and radiates the beloved human being, the contemplated
stone: the soul experiences the unity of the I, and in this unity the
unity of I and world; no longer a "content," but what is infinitely
more than any content.

And yet even this is still not a complete freedom for the soul.
It has received not from itself, but from the other, and the other
is in the hand of the commotion. Thus any incident of the commotion—a thought that transforms the face of the beloved, a cloud
that transforms the face of the rock—can gain power over it and
spoil its unity, so that it stands once again abandoned and enslaved
in the vortex of feelings and objects. And even in the pure moment
itself it can appear as a tearing, as a gazing-out, and instead of the
unity there are two worlds, and the abyss, and the most unsteady
of bridges over it; or chaos, the swarming of darkness that knows
no unity.

But there is an experience which grows in the soul out of the
soul itself, without contact and without restraint, in naked oneness.
It comes into being and completes itself beyond the commotion,
free of the other, inaccessible to the other. It needs no nourishment, and no poison can touch it. The soul which stands in it
stands in itself, has itself, experiences itself—boundlessly. It experiences itself as a unity, no longer because it has surrendered
itself wholly to a thing of the world, gathered itself wholly in a
thing of the world, but because it has submerged itself entirely in
itself, has plunged down to the very ground of itself, is kernel and
husk, sun and eye, carouser and drink, at once. This most inward
of all experiences is what the Greeks call *ek-stasis,* a stepping out.

If religion has really "developed," as people say, then one may
regard as an essential stage of this process the change which the
conception of God has undergone. At first human beings seem to
have explained with the name God primarily that which they did
not understand about the world; then, however, oftener and oftener, that which they did not understand about themselves. Thus

ecstasy—that which humans could least understand about themselves—became God's highest gift.

That phenomenon which one can designate, after an optical concept, as projection, the placing outside of something inward, is demonstrated in its purest form with ecstasy, which, because it is the most inward, is placed the furthest outward. The believer of the Christian age can localize it only at the poles of his cosmos: He must ascribe it to God or to the devil. Jeanne Cambry, who died in 1639, still wrote to her confessor: "I am compelled to make known to you the inner distress in which I have found myself since your last exhortation, since you still leave me in doubt whether it is God or the devil who rules me. If it is the devil, then all the prayer which I have practiced these thirty-seven years is worthless." But not only in those times did people divide life between divine and diabolic because they did not know the power and breadth of the human and failed to grasp the inwardness of ecstasy: there is almost no ecstatic who has not interpreted his I-experience as God-experience (and however they tried to make God inward, scarcely one took him wholly into the I as the unity of the I). This seems to me to be grounded in the nature of the ecstatic experience.

In the experience of ecstasy itself there is as yet nothing that points either inward or outward. Whoever experiences the oneness of I and world knows nothing of I and world. For—as it says in the Upanishads—just as a man embraced by a woman he loves has no consciousness of what is outside or inside, so the mind, embraced by the primal self, has no consciousness of what is outside or inside. But the human being cannot help placing even what is most subjective and free, once it has been lived, in the concatenation of the commotion, and forging for that which, timeless and fetterless as eternity, passed through the soul, a little past (the cause) and a little future (the effect). But the more authentic and unbound the experience is, the harder it necessarily is to place it in the circle of the other, of what is bound—the more natural and irrefutable it is to ascribe it to one who is above the world and outside all bonds. The human being who trudges along day by day in the functions of bodiliness and unfreedom receives in ecstasy a revelation of freedom. One who knows only differentiated experience—the experience of meaning, of thought, of will, connected with one another, yet still separate in this separation, and conscious—comes to know an undifferentiated experience: the experience of the I. One who always feels and knows only particulars about himself suddenly finds himself under the storm cloud of a force, a superabundance, an infinity, in which even the most primal security, the barrier between the self and the other, has foundered. One cannot burden the general run of occurrences with this experience; one does not dare to lay it upon his own poor I, of which he does not suspect that it carries the world-I; so one hangs it on God. And what one thinks, feels and dreams about God then enters into his ecstasies, pours itself out upon them in a shower of images and sounds, and creates around the experience of unity a multiform mystery.

The elementary notion in this mystery is a union—more or less corporeally imagined—with God. Ecstasy is originally an entering into God, *enthusiasmos,* * being filled with the god. Forms of this notion are the eating of the god; inhalation of the divine fire-breath; loving union with the god (this basic form remained characteristic of all later mysticism); being rebegotten, reborn through the god; ascent of the soul to the god, into the god. The Apostle Paul does not know whether his soul was in the body or outside the body, and the Jewish sage, Hai Gaon rejects a popular opinion when he says of the adept who has surmounted the ten rungs of mystical ascent: "Then heaven opens up before him—not in order that he may ascend into it, but something happens in his heart, whereby he enters into the contemplation of things divine." And however long the way that leads from him to the Platonists, to the Sufis, to the German friends of God, the god with whom ecstasy is a union still lives with them too. Only in the most ancient Indian sayings—and perhaps afterward in rare utterances of individuals —is the I proclaimed which is one with the universe, which is unity.

Of all the experiences which are said, in order to mark their incomparability, to be incommunicable, only ecstasy is by its very

---

*Instances of the conception of God as the pneumatic element in which the believer stands are cited in Albrecht Dietrich, ed., *Eine Mithrasliturgie* (Leipzig: B. G. Teubner, 1903) (this book, which is a legacy, must not go unmentioned here); to these we should perhaps add the late-Jewish name for God, "makom," i.e., place, which appears to be the last trace of a primordial image (M. Buber).

nature the ineffable. It is such because the human being who experiences it has become a unity into which no more dualities extend.

What is experienced in ecstasy (if one may really speak of a "what"), is the unity of the I. But in order to be experienced as unity the I must have become a unity. Only one who is completely unified can receive unity. Now it is no longer a bundle, it is a fire. Now the content of its experience and the subject of its experience, world and I, have flowed together. Now all powers have vibrated together into one force, all sparks have blazed together into one flame. Now one is removed from the commotion, removed into the most silent, speechless heavenly kingdom—removed even from language, which the commotion once laboriously created to be its messenger and handmaiden, and which, since the beginning of its existence, desires eternally the one impossible thing: to set its foot on the neck of the commotion and to become all poem—truth, purity, poem.

"Now speaks," as Meister Eckhart says, "the bride in the Song of Songs: 'I climbed over all the mountains and all my faculties, till I reached the dark power of the Father. There I heard without sound, there I saw without light, there I smelt without movement, there I tasted that which was not, there I felt what did not exist. Then my heart became bottomless, my soul loveless, my mind formless and my nature without essence.' Now understand what she means! When she says that she has climbed over all the mountains, she means a transcendence of all speech which she can in any way devise by her own faculties—until she reaches the dark power of the Father, where all speech ends."

Being lifted so completely above the multiplicity of the I, above the play of the senses and of thought, the ecstatic is also separated from language, which cannot follow him. Language came into being as a storing up of signs for the affections and needs of the human body; it grew by forming signs for the palpable things close to the human body or distant from it; it has followed the developing human soul on ever more secret paths and has formed, soldered, chiseled names for the stubbornest of the thousandfold arts and the wildest of the thousandfold mysteries; it has stormed the Olympus of the human mind—no, it has made the Olympus of the human mind by piling up image-word on image-word, until even the highest peak of thought stood in the word. Such things it does and will always do; but always it can receive from only one thing and satisfy only one thing: the sign-begetting plurality of the I. It will never enter the realm of ecstasy, which is the realm of unity.

Language is knowledge—knowledge of nearness or distance, sensation or idea—and knowledge is the work of the commotion, in its greatest miracles a gigantic coordinate system of the mind. But the experience of ecstasy is not a knowing.

That is the meaning of what we read in the book of Hierotheos (the Syrian Stefan bar Sudaili?)—the same Hierotheos, as far as we can judge, of whom it is said in the Areopagitic writings that he not only came to know God, but also suffered him—οὐ μόνον μαθὼν ἀλλὰ καὶ παθὼν τα θἔια—"It seems right to me to say without words and to understand without knowledge that which is above words and knowledge: by this I mean nothing other than the secret silence and the mystic peace that annihilates consciousness and dissolves forms. Then seek, in the silence and in the mystery, that complete and original union with the essential and primal good."

But not merely in comparison to his early plurality has the one who has experienced ecstasy become a unity. One's unity is not relative, not limited by the other; it is limitless, for it is the unity of I and world. One's unity is solitude, absolute solitude: the solitude of that which is without limits. One contains the other, the others in oneself, in one's unity: as world; but one no longer has others *outside* oneself, no longer has any communion with them or anything in common with them. But language is a function of community, and it can say nothing except what is held in common. It must somehow transfer even what is most personal into the common experience of human beings, must somehow compound the personal out of the common experience in order to express it. Ecstasy stands beyond the common experience. It is unity, solitude, uniqueness: that which cannot be transferred. It is the abyss that cannot be fathomed: the unsayable.

In that passage of the great Parisian magic book* that contains

---

*The reference is to the so-called Great Magical Codex of Paris (papyrus 574 of the Biblioteque Nationale). For a German translation see A. Dietrich, *Eine Mithras-liturgie* (see p. 4 note). An English translation is to be published by Hans Dieter Betz in his forthcoming volume, *Greek Magical Papyri* (The University of Chicago Press) (editor's note).

the Apathanatismos, the mystic's guide to the highest initiation, one is told: "But you will see how the gods turn their gaze upon you and come against you by storm. You, however, shall at once lay your forefinger upon your mouth and say: 'Silence, Silence, Silence—*symbolon* of the living, everlasting God—protect me, Silence!' . . . And when you behold the higher world, pure and solitary, with no god or angel stormily advancing, prepare yourself to hear a crashing of mighty thunder, which will cause you to tremble. You, however, shall say again: 'Silence.' Grant this: I am a star that travels with you along your paths and shines upward from the depths."

Silence is our *symbolon* which protects us from the gods and angels of the commotion, our guard against its aberrations, our purification against its impurity. We ensilence the experience, and it is a star that travels along its path. We speak it, and it is thrown down under the tread of the market. When we are quiet to the Lord, he makes his dwelling with us; we say Lord, Lord, and we have lost him. But that is how it is with us: We have to speak. And our speech builds a heaven over us, over us and the others a vault of heaven: poetry, love, future. But one thing is not beneath this heaven: the one thing that is needful.

Consciousness puts ecstasy outside, in projection; the will puts it outside again in the attempt to say the unsayable. Even the innermost experience is not kept safe from the drive to expression. I believe in ecstasies that were never touched by a sound, as in an invisible sanctuary of humanity; the documents of those that flowed into words are before me. Here are human beings who could not bear their solitude, the highest, the absolute solitude, who climbed out of the infinite they had experienced into the midst of the finite, from unity into the midst of the teeming multiplicity. As soon as they spoke—as soon as they talked to themselves, in the usual prelude to speech—they were already in chains, in bounds; the unbounded ones do not speak even to themselves, in themselves, because there are no boundaries within them either: no multiplicity, no duality, no more Thou in the I. They speak, and already they are betrayed to language, which is adequate to everything, only not to the ground of experience, which is oneness. They say, and already they say *the other thing.*

True, there is another, most silent speech, which wants not to describe existence, but only to communicate it. It is so high and still as if it were not in language, but like a lifting of the eyelids in silence. It commits no betrayal, for it says only that something is.

That knowledgeable orator and churchman, Bernard de Clairvaux, halts suddenly for once in the midst of his sermon and says softly, without boasting and without being humble, it is no artistic device, rather memory has come over him, and speech has broken in his mouth: *Fateor et mihi adventasse verbum:* I confess that the Word has approached me too. Thereupon he continues speaking, a little louder perhaps, but still resisting the importunity of Art, which wants to come in again: how he felt that it was there, how he recalls its having been there, how he sensed that it would come, yet did not feel its coming and going. How it could not enter through any sense, being non-sensible, and how it could not have originated in him, being perfect. "When I gazed out, I found it beyond all that was outside me; when I looked in, it was further in than my most inward being. And I recognized that what I had read was true: that we live and move and are in it; but he is blest in whom it lives, who is moved by it." I believe his confession. I feel that once, at a time when he could not speak as today, he had hours when he too suffered the divine. And all the adroit elegance of his speech is purchased, in my eyes, by the fact that he reports his hour in this way, that he does not fling down the Word as fodder for the words, but bears witness for the Word with his silence as a martyr bears witness with his blood.

From this speaking many gradations lead to those narrations of God and his gifts, narrations that do not take fright and turn back, but say and say. They are not less honest; nowhere does their language sound as if it had a crack in it; we know that they are not lying, but confessing something they mean. But stillness is lacking, and where there is no stillness the voice of necessity has the ring of arbitrariness.

Even the phenomenon of projection itself—that someone who has experienced his I announces to himself and others that he has experienced God—must appear arbitrary to many: To the godless it seems the arbitrariness of a superfluous theism (or impure pantheism); to the pious it seems the arbitrariness of presumption and blasphemy. "And when they," says Jeremy Taylor, the seventeenth century English bishop, too subtle a spirit for indignation in place of understanding, "suffer raptures beyond the burdens and supports of reason, they suffer they know not what, and call it what they please." And yet it is in truth not arbitrary; it is urgency and necessity.

And still more arbitrary seems the content of the confession of the ecstatic, especially when he has not experienced in his own soul the tragedy that takes place when the drive for expression of the innermost and most personal meets the given language of human beings: that battle of the irrational with the rational, which ends without victory or defeat, in a scrap of paper with writing on it, which to the seeing eye bears the seal of a great suffering.

The seventeenth century French prelate Bossuet, whose mind is of a lesser order than Taylor's and who fancies logic (as long as it does not interfere with dogma), would like to annihilate the ecstatic by wittily exposing his contradiction. They say, he exclaims, that contemplation excludes not only all images in memory and all traces in the brain, but every idea and every mental phenomenon; and even as they say this, they are forced to tear it down, not only with respect to mental phenomena and ideas, but even with respect to corporeal images, for the books in which they exclude them are full of them.

Indeed, a contradiction has been uncovered. But what can it mean for the judgment of human beings who spend their lives in the torment of a monstrous contradiction: the contradiction between the inner experience *(Erlebnis)* and the commotion out of which they ascended, only to fall back into it again and again? That is the contradiction between ecstasy, which does not go into memory, and the desire to save it for memory, in the image, in speech, in confession.

Yes, it is true: the ecstatic cannot say the unsayable. He says the other thing—images, dreams, visions—not unity. He speaks, he must speak, because the Word burns in him. The one who did not speak to humans did speak to himself; he was more holy, because outwardly he remained solitary, but perhaps he remained solitary because he was not so stricken and driven to bear the message to others, the impossible message?

He does not lie who speaks of unity in images, dreams, visions, who stammer of unity. Forms and sounds which, born of his feeling for God, circled around the primal experience, have remained in his memory: around the driving conflagration which remains in him as sole trace of the experience; perhaps other forms and sounds, surfacing from darker spheres of his soul, get themselves mixed in; he grasps at them, not knowing where they come from, in order to understand himself. For he does not understand himself; and yet the desire to understand himself, which in ecstasy was extinguished, has awakened in him. He says the forms and sounds and notices that he is not saying the experience, not the ground, not the unity, and would like to stop himself and cannot, and feels the impossibility of saying it, like a seven-locked gate which he rattles, knowing that it will never open, yet he must go on rattling it. For the Word burns in him. Ecstasy is dead, stabbed in the back by Time, which will not be mocked; but, dying, it has flung the Word into him, and the Word burns in him. And he speaks, speaks, he cannot be silent, the flame in the Word drives him, he knows that he cannot say it, yet he tries over and over again until his soul is exhausted to death and the Word leaves him. This is the *exaltatio* of the one who has returned into the commotion and cannot resign himself to it; this is his insurrection, the insurrection of a speaker: related to the insurrection of the poet, slighter in possession, mightier in existence, than his. This is the bending of the bow for the saying of the unsayable, an impossible task, a labor in the dark. Its work, the confession, bears its mark.

And yet the ecstatic's will to say is not mere impotence and stammering; it is also might and mastery. He wants to create a memorial for ecstasy which leaves no traces, to tow the timeless into the harbor of time; he wants to make the unity without multiplicity into the unity of all multiplicity. The thought of the great myth awakens, a thought which runs through all the times of humanity: the myth of unity which becomes plurality because it wants to gaze and be gazed at, to know and be known, to love and be loved, and which, while itself remaining unity, embraces itself as multiplicity; of the I which begets a Thou; of the primal self which transforms itself into the world, of the divinity which transforms itself into God. Is the myth proclaimed by Vedas and Upanishads, Midrash and Kabbala, Plato and Jesus, not the symbol of what the ecstatic has experienced? Did not the masters of all times, who created and recreated it again and again, draw on their own experience? For they too have experienced unity; and they too passed out of unity into multiplicity. But because their ecstasy was not the irruption of something unheard of, overwhelming the soul, but an ingathering and deep upwelling and a familiarity with the ground, the Word did not lie upon them like a driving conflagration; it lay upon them like the hand of a father. And so it guided them to insert the experience—not as an event in the commotion, nor as a report in the intelligence of time, but to put it into the deed of their lives, to work it into their work, to make of it the new poem of the primal myth, and thus to place it not as a thing among the things of the earth, but as a star amid the stars of heaven.

But is the myth a phantasm? Is it not a revelation of the ultimate reality of being? Is not the experience of the ecstatic a symbol of the primal experience of the universal mind? Are not both a living, inner experience?

We listen to our inmost selves—and do not know which sea we hear murmuring.

—Martin Buber

India

PRINCE DARA SHEKOH AND THE ASCETIC BABA LAL

FROM THEIR CONVERSATIONS IN THE GARDENS OF JAFFER KHAN
SUDAH IN 1649, WRITTEN DOWN BY A KSHATRIYA AND A BRAHMAN
ATTACHED TO THE PRINCE'S RETINUE

The prince: How do the supreme soul and the living soul differ?

The ascetic: They do not differ, and pleasure and pain, which are ascribed to the living soul, arise from its imprisonment in the body. The water of the Ganges is the same, whether it run in the riverbed or be poured into a decanter.

The prince: What difference can this create?

The ascetic: A difference: A drop of water added to the water in the decanter will impart its flavor to the whole, but it would be lost in the river. The higher soul, therefore, is without accident, but the living soul is afflicted by sense and passion. Water cast loosely on a fire will extinguish the fire; put that water over the fire in a boiler, and the fire will vaporize the water. So the body is the confining caldron; passion the fire; and the soul, the water, is dispersed abroad. The one great supreme soul is incapable of these properties, and happiness is therefore only obtained in reunion with it, when the dispersed and individualized portions combine with it, as the drops of water with the parent stream. Hence, although God needs not the service of his slave, yet the slave should remember that he is separated from God by the body alone, and may well exclaim perpetually: Blessed be the moment when I shall lift the veil off that face. The veil of the face of my beloved is the dust of my body.

The prince: What are the feelings of the perfect fakir?

The ascetic: They have not been, they are not to be described, as it is said: A person asked me what are the sensations of a lover? I replied: When you are a lover, you will know.

RAMAKRISHNA (1833–1886)

FROM HIS LIFE, ACCORDING TO THE NOTES OF HIS DISCIPLE
VIVEKANANDA

He began to look upon the image of the goddess Kali as his mother and the mother of the universe. He believed it to be living and breathing and taking food out of his hand. After the regular forms of worship he would sit there for hours and hours, singing hymns and talking and praying to her as a child to his mother, till he lost all consciousness of the outward world. Sometimes he would weep for hours and would not be comforted, because he could not see his mother as perfectly as he wished. . . . His whole soul, as it were, melted into one flood of tears, and he appealed to the goddess to have mercy on him and reveal herself to him. . . . Crowds assembled round him and tried to console him, when the blowing of the conch shells proclaimed the death of another day, and he gave vent to his sorrow, saying, "Mother, oh my mother, another day has gone, and still I have not found thee." . . .

One day as he was feeling his separation from the goddess very keenly and thinking of putting an end to himself, as he could no longer bear his loneliness, he lost all outward sensation and saw his mother (Kali) in a vision. These visions came to him again and again, and then he became calmer. . . .

These visions grew more and more, and his trances became longer and longer, till everyone saw that it was no longer possible for him to perform his daily course of duties. For instance, it is prescribed in the Shastras that a man should put a flower over his own head and think of himself as the very god or goddess he is going to worship; and Ramakrishna, as he put the flower over his head and thought of himself as identified with his mother, would get entranced and would remain in that state for hours. Then again, from time to time, he would entirely lose his own identity, so much so as to appropriate to himself the offerings brought for the goddess. Sometimes, forgetting to adorn the image, he would adorn himself with the flowers. . . .

The ardent soul of Ramakrishna could not remain quiet with these frequent visions, but ran eagerly to attain perfection and realization of God in all his different aspects. He thus began the twelve years of unheard of *tapasya,* or ascetic exercises. Looking back to these years of self-torture in his later days, he said that a religious tornado had raged within him and made everything topsy-turvy. He had no idea then that it had lasted for so long a time. He never had a wink of sound sleep during these years, could not even doze, but his eyes would remain always open and fixed. He thought sometimes that he was seriously ill, and holding a looking glass before him, he put his finger within the sockets of his eyes, that the lids might close, but they would not. In his despair he would cry out: "Mother, oh! my mother, is this the fruit of calling upon thee and believing in thee?" And at once a sweet voice would come, and a still sweeter smiling face, and would say: "My son! how could you hope to realize the highest truth if you don't give up the love of your body and of your little self?"

"A torrent of spiritual light" [Buber: life], he said, "would come then, deluging my mind and urging me forward. I used to tell my mother, 'Mother! I could never learn from these erring humans, but I will learn from thee, and thee alone,' and the same voice would say, 'Yea, my son!' I did not even look to the preservation of my body. My hair grew till it became matted, and I had no idea of it. My nephew Hridaya used to bring me some food daily; some days he succeeded, and some days he did not succeed, in forcing a few mouthfuls down my throat, though I had no idea of it. Sometimes I used to go to the closet of the servants and sweepers and clean it with my own hands, and pray, 'Mother! destroy in me all idea that I am great, and that I am a Brahman, and that they are low and pariahs, for who are they but thou in so many forms?' " . . .

A *sannyasin* (ascetic) could not understand Ramakrishna's love for his mother (the goddess). He would talk of it as mere superstition and ridicule it. Thereupon Ramakrishna gave him to understand that in the Absolute there is no thou, nor I, nor God, that it is beyond all speech or thought. As long, however, as there is the least grain of relativity left, the Absolute is within thought and speech and within the limits of the mind, which mind is subservient to the universal mind and consciousness; and this omniscient, universal consciousness was to him his mother and God.

He began to practice and realize the Vaishnava idea of love for God. This love, according to the Vaishnavas, becomes manifest in any one of the following relations: the relation of servant to master; of friend to friend; of child to parents, or vice versa; and of wife to husband. The highest point of love is reached when the human soul can love God as a wife loves her husband. The shepherdess of Braja had this sort of love toward the divine Krishna, and there was no thought of any carnal relationship. No one, they say, can understand this love of Sri Radha and Sri Krishna until he is perfectly free of all carnal desires. They even prohibit ordinary people to read the books that treat of this love of Radha and Krishna, because they are still under the sway of passion. Ramakrishna, in order to realize this love, dressed himself in women's attire for several days, thought of himself as a woman, and at last succeeded in gaining his ideal. He saw the beautiful form of Sri Krishna in a trance and was satisfied.

In his later days he was thinking of practicing the tenets of Christianity. He had seen Jesus in a vision, and for three days he could think of nothing and speak of nothing but Jesus and his love. There was this peculiarity in all his visions—that he always saw them outside himself, but when they vanished they seemed to have entered into him.

He was a wonderful mixture of God and man. In his ordinary state he would talk of himself as a servant of all men and women. He saw them all as God [Buber: as the god]. He himself would never be addressed as guru, or teacher. Never would he claim for himself any high position. He would touch the ground reverently where his pupils had trodden. But every now and then strange fits of God-consciousness came upon him. He then became changed into a different being altogether. He spoke of himself as being able to do and know everything. He spoke as if he had the power to give anything to anybody. He would speak of himself as the same soul that had formerly been born as Rama, as Krishna, as Jesus, or as Buddha, reborn as Ramakrishna. He told Mathuranatha, long before anyone knew him, that he had many disciples who would come to him shortly and that he knew all of them. He said that he was free from all eternity, and his religious exercises and exertions were only meant to show the people the way to salvation. He had done all for them alone. He would say he was a Nitya-mukta, or eternally free, and an incarnation of God himself. "The fruit of the pumpkin," he said, "comes out first, and then the flowers; so it is with the Nitya-muktas, or those who are free from all eternity, but come down for the good of others."

SAYINGS OF RAMAKRISHNA

★ Many are the names of God, and infinite the forms that lead us to know him. In whatsoever name or form you desire to call him, in that very form and name you will see him.

★ As many have heard of snow but have not seen it, so many are the religious preachers who have read only in books about the attributes of God, but have not realized them in their lives. And as many have seen but not tasted it, so many are the religious teachers who have only a glimpse of divine glory, but have not understood its real essence. One who has tasted the snow can say what it is like. One who has enjoyed the society of God in different aspects, now as a servant, now as a friend, now as a lover, or as being absorbed in him, can alone tell what are the attributes of God.

★ At a certain stage of the path of devotion, the devotee finds satisfaction in the God with form; at another stage, in the God without form.

★ As long as someone cries out "Allah Ho! Allah Ho!" (O God! O God!), be sure that he has not found God, for whoever has found him becomes still.

★ A logician asked Sri Ramakrishna, "What are knowledge, the knower, and the object known?" Whereupon he answered, "Good man, I do not know all these niceties of scholastic learning. I know only my Mother divine, and that I am her son."

★ The knowledge of God may be likened to a man, while the love of God is likened to a woman. Knowledge has entry only up to the outer rooms of God; but no one can enter into the inner mysteries of God save a lover, for to such a one, as to a woman, even the most secret chambers are open.

★ God is in all humans, but all humans are not in God; that is the reason why they suffer.

★ He spoke to those women whom society would not touch: "Mother, in one form thou art in the street, and in another form thou art the universe. I salute thee, Mother, I salute thee."

★ I see, I experience, that all three come from *one* wisdom— the sacrifice, the altar, and the offerer.

★ Mother, I am the tool, you are the worker, I am the chamber, you are the tenant, I am the sheath, you are the sword, I am the chariot, you are the charioteer.

★ The human being is perfected by realizing the following states: First, all this is I; second, all this is you; third, you are the master, I am the servant.

★ One who loves God desires to enjoy the society of God, not to become one with him. One's desire is not to be transformed into the sugar, but to taste it.

★ When he was on his deathbed and could scarcely speak or swallow, he said, "I speak and eat now with so many mouths."

BAYEZID BISTAMI (ninth century)

The following words of Bayezid are related:

"For twelve years at a stretch I was the smith of my own being. I laid it on the hearth of asceticism, heated it red-hot in the fire of ordeals, set it on the anvil of fear, and pounded it with the hammer of admonition. Thus I made it into a mirror that served me to gaze at myself for five years, during which I never ceased to dissolve the rust from this mirror by acts of piety and devotion."

Moreover he said, "For thirty years I went in search of God, and when at the end of that time I opened my eyes, I discovered that it was he who had been looking for me."

He said, "For thirty years the exalted Lord was my mirror, now I am my own mirror."

Yahya, who desired to see Bayezid, set out on the way to him, but did not find him at home, for at that time he was among the graves, occupied with acts of worship. It was the hour of evening prayer. Yahya went to look for Bayezid and soon found him. He said to himself, "Now it is night, but tomorrow early I will salute him." Until the first rays of dawn he saw Bayezid standing upright on his feet, murmuring words, and was astonished. When the sun rose, Yahya went to salute Bayezid. "What were you doing all last night?" he asked him.

"Last night," answered Bayezid, "I was shown twenty degrees, none of which I accepted, for they were all curtains that kept me from going forward."

Then Yahya said, "Oh Bayezid! Give me some advice."

"Very well," said Bayezid, "even if you should be offered the degree that all the prophets attained, do not consent to accept it. Demand to go further; keep raising your demands. For if you accept a degree, it will become a curtain for you, and will hold you back."

Bayezid said to Ahmed Khizreviyeh, "How long will you keep pacing the world in all directions?"

"When the flow of water is damned at any point," said Ahmed, "it becomes stagnant."

"Then be like the ocean," said Bayezid, "and you won't become stagnant."

Bayezid said, "When I had reached the level of nearness, I heard someone calling, 'O Bayezid! Demand all you have to demand.' 'My God,' I answered, 'it is you I demand.' I heard, 'O Bayezid! As long as the tiniest mote of worldly desire remains in you and you have not yet reached the level of decreation and become nothing, you will not be able to find us.' 'My God,' I said, 'that I may not return from your court empty-handed, I would demand something of you.' 'Very well then, demand it.' 'Grant me the pardon for all humankind, and have mercy on them.' A voice rang out, 'O Bayezid! Lift up your eyes!' I lifted up my eyes and saw that the exalted Lord was still more moved to clemency toward his servants than I was. 'My God,' I cried then, 'bestow your mercy on Satan!' 'O Bayezid!' the voice answered me, 'Satan is made of fire, and fire needs fire.' "

When someone asked him his age, he answered that he was four years old.

"How so, O sheikh?"

"For seventy years I was enveloped in the veil of the lower world, and it is only four years since I became free of it and can see God."

One night in a dream I saw the Lord, who said to me, "What do you desire, Bayezid?"

"That which you desire, my God!"

"O Bayezid, it is you I desire, as you desire me."
"But what is the way that leads to you?"
"O Bayezid, whoever renounces himself comes to me."

Bayezid said, "I am like an ocean without beginning, without end, without bottom."

Bayezid was asked what the ninth heaven is. "I am the ninth heaven," he answered.
"And the throne that rests thereon?"
"I am that too," he said. When the questioner continued asking, he said, "I am the tablet, I am the stylus. I am Abraham, Moses, Jesus. I am Gabriel, Michael, Israfil. Whoever comes into true being is dissolved in God, is God."

Bayezid said, "When the exalted Lord in his generous mercy had raised me to the higher levels, he illumined with his beams my entire outer and inner being, unveiled to me all his secrets and manifested in me all his greatness. . . . When the exalted Lord, annihilating my temporal being, allowed me to participate in his unending duration, the clarity of my eye was sharpened even to infallibility. I saw God with God's eye; I saw God through God; and entrenching myself in the truth, I remained calm and at peace. I closed the opening of my ear, I drew my tongue back into my helpless mouth, and I threw away the borrowed knowledge which I had learned from the creatures. Thanks to the aid of the exalted Lord I removed my sensual being from myself, and with renewed favor the Lord gave me the knowledge that has no beginning. Through his generosity he has set a tongue in my mouth that can speak and has given me an eye made of his own light."

Bayezid said, "How long will there be I and thou between me and thee? Abolish my I, which stands between us, so that I may dissolve in you completely and become nothing. My God, when I am with you I am worth more than anyone, and when I am with myself I am worth less than anyone. My God, the practices of holy poverty and unrelenting strictness have made it possible for me to come to you. In your generosity you have not willed that my efforts should come to nothing. My God, it is not asceticism that I need, not knowledge of the Koran by heart, and not science; but give me a share in your mysteries. My God, I seek my refuge in you, and it is through you that I come to you. My God, it is not astonishing that I love you, for I am your servant, weak, helpless, needy; but it is strange that you love me, you, the King of Kings! My God, now I fear you, and yet I love you with such great ardor! How shall I love you once I have received my portion of your mercy and my heart is free of all fear."

He said, "I went from God to God, until they cried out from me into me, 'O thou I!' "

HUSSEIN AL HALLADJ (D. 309 H-922 C.E.)

At the festival on the slope of Mount Arfat he said, "O thou signpost for the dull witted!" And when he saw all the people praying, he climbed a hill and watched them, and as they were all coming back he struck himself and cried out, "Thou exalted Lord, I know thou art pure, and I say thou art pure of all the praise of the praisers and all the worship of the worshippers and all the thoughts of the thinkers. My God! Thou knowest that I cannot fulfill the obligation of praise. Praise thou thyself in my stead, that is the true praise."

He was asked whether a contemplative has time left over for himself. "No," he said, "Time expresses the state of one who needs times for enlightenment; but whoever cannot be content with his state is a knower. That is, one must be able to say, in the words of Mohammed, 'I have times with God when no angel, no cherub even, can grasp me.' "

He was asked, "What is the way to God?" He answered, "Pull back both your feet, and you will be with him—one foot from out of this life, the other foot from out of the other life."

Likewise he said, "Knowing means seeing things, but also being submerged, like all things, in the Absolute."

He said, "When the servant has arrived at the rung of knowledge, God sends him an inspiration, his joy becomes dull, and nothing is to his taste any longer, except the enjoyment of God."

Moreover he said, "The gaze of the seers, the knowledge of the knowers, the light of those who know in the spirit, and the way of those who make swift progress, and the eternity of Before and the eternity of After and all that lies between are temporality." And how do we know this? Hussein answers, "Whoever has a heart, let him throw away his eye, then he will see."

Likewise, "Whosoever seeks God sits in the shadow of his penitence, but whomsoever God seeks sits in the shadow of his innocence."

Likewise, "Whosoever seeks God runs ahead of his revelations, but whomsoever God seeks has revelations that overtake his running."

Likewise, "Hours of divine enlightenment are shells that lie in the sea of our hearts; the morning of resurrection casts them up on shore, and they spring open."

He said, "I am the one I love, and the one I love is I; we are two souls fused in one body. When you see me, you see him. When you see him, you see us."

Now when people began to be astonished at him, liars without judgment revealed themselves, and also many adherents. Wonderful things were seen of him. Some whetted their tongues to calumny and brought his sayings before the caliph. The Imams of Baghdad also voted to condemn him to death, because he had said, "I am God!" They demanded that he should say, "He is God!" He replied, "Yes, everything is he! You say that he is submerged [in the beings], but Hussein is submerged; the ocean does not become submerged, nor does it annihilate."

On the way to his execution he danced, flinging his hands about like a high-spirited stallion, though laden with sixteen chains. They said, "What sort of going is this?" He answered, "Am I not going to my place of sacrifice?" Thereupon he uttered a loud cry and sang these verses:

Never would I wish my friend to be accused of cruelty.
He handed me what he drinks himself, as a host to a guest.
But as the cups went round he called for the block and the sword.
So it fares with him who drinks wine with the dragon in the heat of
  summer.

FERID ED-DIN ATTAR (ca. 1120–1220)

"THE SEVEN VALLEYS" FROM THE "CONFERENCE OF THE BIRDS"

The first valley that presents itself is the Valley of Seeking; after that comes the Valley of Love, which has no boundaries; the third is that of Knowledge; the fourth that of Self-Sufficiency; the fifth that of pure Unity; the sixth that of Consternation; and the seventh and last is the Valley of Dissolution and Annihilation, beyond which you cannot go. You will feel yourself drawn on, yet you will be unable to progress further; a single drop of water will be like a sea to you.

The Valley of Seeking

As soon as you enter the Valley of Seeking, hundredfold torment will attack you again and again. In every moment you will undergo a hundred ordeals; there the parrot of the firmament* is no more than a fly. In this valley you will pass many years in laborious tension and constant transformation of your condition. You will have to leave your treasure behind and stake everything you possess on the game. You will have to wade in a river of blood, resign yourself to total renunciation. And when you have acquired the certainty that you possess nothing more, you must still detach your heart from all that is. Once it is freed from every appearance of separation, the divine glory will blaze up before it, and through this light's revealing itself to you, your desire will grow to infinity.

And though a fire should appear in the path of the wanderer, and though a thousand chasms, each more impassable than the last, should yawn, still he, impelled by longing, would forge on into the chasms like a madman, plunge into the flames like a moth. Driven by love's folly, he will live for the search; he will demand a drink from his cupbearer. Once he has drunk a few drops of this wine, he will forget both worlds. Submerged in the sea of the limitless, he will feel that his lips are dry, and in the depths of his own self he will inquire into the secret of eternal beauty. In his desire to know it, he will not retreat before the dragons who devour souls. If belief and unbelief were to step up to him at this moment, he would welcome both alike, provided they would only

---

*The Persian calls the sky green rather than blue (M. Buber).

open the gate for him. Once this gate is open, what is belief or unbelief, since on the other side of the entrance neither one nor the other exists? . . .

Huddled like a child in the lap of its mother, gather yourself in yourself, immersed in blood. Do not leave your inwardness in order to get yourself to the outer world. If you need victual, nourish yourself on blood. Blood alone nourishes the child in its mother's womb; and it comes from the warmth of inwardness. . . .

The Valley of Love

In order to enter here, one must immerse oneself entirely in fire; indeed one must oneself be fire, else one could not live. The true lover must be like fire, with a blazing countenance, burning and furious as fire. To love, one must have no mental reservations; one must be prepared to throw a hundred worlds into the fire; one must know neither belief nor unbelief, harbor neither doubt nor confidence. Upon this way there is no difference between good and evil; where there is love, good and evil have vanished. . . .

In this valley love is the fire, and its smoke is reason. When love comes, reason flees hastily away. Reason cannot live with love's ravings; love has nothing to do with human reason. Only if you could get a good look at the invisible world could you recognize the source of the mysterious love which I proclaim to you. The existence of love is destroyed, petal by petal, by the intoxication of love itself.

The Valley of Knowledge

When the sun of knowledge beams from the vault of this path, which cannot be described in terms worthy of it, . . . the mystery of the being of things appears with clarity, and the fiery furnace of the world becomes a flower garden. The wanderer will see the almond beneath its shell.* He will see himself no longer; he will see nothing more, save his friend alone; in everything he sees he will see his friend's face, in every atom the sphere of the universe; beneath the veil he will contemplate countless mysteries that shine like the sun. . . . The visible world and the invisible world are

---

*That is, God in the creatures (M. Buber).

nothing to the soul; the body is not hidden from the soul, nor the soul from the body. Once you have left the world that is nothing, you will find the place that is destined for the human being. . . .

The Valley of Self-Sufficiency

Here there is no passion and no searching. Out of this willingness of the soul to rely on itself a cold storm arises whose might devastates enormous spaces in the twinkling of an eye. The seven oceans are then no more than a puddle of water; the seven planets, a spark; the seven heavens, a curtain; the seven hells, a shattered ice block. . . .

If you were to see a whole world whose heart was being devoured by fire, you would merely be having a dream. The thousands of souls that ceaselessly sink down beside this sea are nothing but a light and imperceptible dew. . . .

This valley is not as easy to pass through as you, in your simplicity, might believe. Even if your heart's blood were to pour into this sea, you could reach only the first station. And if you were to stride down all the world's roads, still, when you paused to consider, you would find yourself at the first step. Indeed no wanderer has seen the goal of his journey and found the cure for his love. If you stop moving you will turn to stone, or die and become a corpse. If you put one foot before the other and keep striding forward, to all eternity you will hear the cry, "Onward!" You are not permitted to progress nor to stand still; it will not profit you either to live or to die. What gain have you gotten from all the toil you have borne? It is all the same whether you beat yourself on the head or not, O you who hear me! Be still, leave all this and act. . . .

Try to be independent and self-sufficient. . . . In this fourth valley the lightning of the virtue of self-reliance flashes so strongly that its warmth consumes hundreds of worlds. Since hundreds of worlds turn to dust, would it be extraordinary if the world we inhabit also disappeared? . . . In this valley no one may remain idle, and only the mature may enter. Now it is time to act, instead of remaining in uncertainty or frivolity: Get up, then, and traverse this toilsome valley, having renounced your mind and your heart; for if you have not renounced both of them you are committing idolatry, and the most frivolous of idolatries. Therefore sacrifice your mind and heart on this path; otherwise you must give up all hope of being self-sufficient. . . .

The Valley of Unity

This is the place where all things are laid bare and unified. All those who lift their heads in this wilderness, draw them out of the same collar. Even if you see many individual beings, there are in reality only a few; no, there is only one. Since the crowds of persons in reality make only one, this one is perfect in its unity. But what presents itself to you as a unity is no different from that which is counted. Since the being I proclaim is outside this unity and outside numbers, leave off speculating about the eternity of Before and the eternity of After; and since both eternities have run out, remember them no more. . . .

Once the wanderer enters this valley, he will disappear, like the earth under his feet. He will be lost, for the single being will be revealed. He will be mute, for the single being will speak. The part will become the whole, or rather it will be neither part nor whole. It will be a form without body and soul. . . . What is the intellect? It has remained on the threshold of the gate, like a child born blind. Whoever has found something of this mystery will turn his head away from the kingdoms of both worlds. . . . The being I proclaim does not exist separately; the whole world is this being; whether it is or is not, it is still this being. . . .

The Valley of Consternation

The Valley of Unity is followed by that of Consternation. There one is the prey of gloom and groaning. There the sighs are like swords, and every breath is a bitter lament. There nothing is save wailing, sorrow, and consuming heat; there it is day and night at once, and that is neither day nor night. There one can see blood drip from the end of each hair, without its being cut off. . . . How will the person, in consternation, be able to go on? He will be stunned and lose himself along the way. But whoever has unity engraved upon his heart, forgets everything and forgets himself. When asked, "Are you or are you not; have you the feeling of being or not; are you in the center or on the periphery; are you visible or hidden; are you transient or immortal; are you the one and the other or neither the one nor the other; are you yourself or not yourself?" he will answer, "I know nothing of it, I am ignorant of it, and ignorant of myself. I am in love, but I do not know with whom; I am neither faithful nor unfaithful. What am I, then? I am ignorant even of my love; my heart is full of love and empty of love at the same time. . . ."

Whoever enters the Valley of Consternation enters at every moment into so great a pain that it would be enough to afflict a hundred worlds. But how much longer shall I endure the affliction and confusion of the mind? Having gone astray, where shall I go? I know not, but may it please God that I may know! . . .

The Valley of Dissolution and Annihilation

It is impossible to describe this valley. Oblivion, muteness, deafness and powerlessness are to be considered as its essential condition. There you see the thousand eternal shadows that surround you disappearing in a single sunbeam.

When the sea of infinity begins to stir up its waves, how shall the images that were traced on its surface endure? These images are the present world and the coming world. Whosoever pronounces that they do not exist has acquired greatness. Whosoever has lost his heart in this sea is lost in it forever and remains in quiet. . . .

An impure object may fall into a sea of rose water, yet it will remain in worthlessness because of its character. But when a pure thing falls into this sea, it will lose its particular existence; it will participate in the motion of the waves; by ceasing to exist separately, it will begin to be beautiful. It is and is not. How can this happen? It is impossible for the mind to grasp it. . . .

Whosoever has left the world in order to follow this path finds death, and after death immortality. . . .

Wrap yourself in the cloak of nothingness and drink from the cup of annihilation, cover your breast with the love of vanishing away, and set the burnoose of nonbeing on your head. Set your foot in the stirrup of unconditional renunciation and resolutely spur your steed to the place where nothing is. In the center and outside the center, under it, over it, in unity, gird your loins with the belt of decreation. Open your eyes and look; put blue salve upon your eyes. If you wish to be lost, you will be lost in a moment, and then again in a different manner; but you shall stride on calmly, until you come to the realm of abolition. If you possess so much as the end of a hair from this world, you will never receive tidings from that world. If the slightest egoism remains in you, then for you the seven oceans will be full of bane. . . .

Throw everything you have into the fire, even your shoes. When you have nothing more, think not even of a shroud and throw yourself naked into the fire. . . .

When your inner being is collected in renunciation, then you will be beyond good and evil. When there is neither good nor evil for you, only then will you love and be finally worthy of salvation, which is the work of love. . . .

As for me, who have remained neither myself nor someone other than myself . . . I have completely lost my way, far from myself; I find in my situation no salvation save despair. When the sun of dissolution rose and shone over me, it burned up both worlds as easily as a grain of millet. When I saw the rays of that sun, I did not remain separate: The drop of water has returned to the sea. Although in my game I have sometimes won and sometimes lost, at the last I cast all into the black water. I have been wiped out; I have disappeared; nothing has remained of me. I had been reduced to a shadow; not the tiniest mote of me existed. I was a drop lost in the ocean of mystery, and now I cannot even find this drop any more.

JALAL AL-DIN RUMI (1207–1273)

FROM THE MASNAVI

> At times my state resembles a dream,
> My dreaming seems to them infidelity.
> Know my eyes sleep, but my heart is awake;
> My body, though torpid, is instinct with energy. . . .
> Your eyes are awake and your heart fast asleep,
> My eyes are closed, and my heart is at the "open door."
> My hearing has five other senses of its own;
> These senses of my heart view the two worlds.
> Let not a weakling like you censure me,
> What seems night to you is broad day to me;
> What seems a prison to you is a garden to me,

Busiest occupation is rest to me.
Your feet are in the mire; to me the mire is transformed to roses,
What to you is funeral wailing is marriage drum to me.
While I seem on earth, abiding with you in the house,
I ascend like Saturn to the seventh heaven.
'Tis not I who companion with you, 'tis my shadow;
My exaltation transcends your thoughts,
Because I have transcended thought,
Yea, I have sped beyond reach of thought.
I am lord of thought, not overlorded by thought,
As the builder is lord of the building.
All creatures are enslaved to thought;
For this cause they are sad at heart and sorrowful.
I send myself on an embassy to thought,
And, at will, spring back again from thought.
I am as the bird of heaven and thought is the fly;
How can the fly lend a helping hand to me?

From the Divan

What is to be done, O Moslems? For I do not recognize myself.
I am neither Christian, nor Jew, nor Parsi, nor Moslem.
I am not of the East, nor of the West, nor of the land, nor of the sea;
I am not of Nature's workshop, nor of the circling heavens.
I am not of earth, nor of water, nor of air, nor of fire;
I am not of the Heavenly City, nor of the dust, nor of existence, nor
    of entity.
I am not of this world, nor of the next, nor of Paradise, nor of Hell;
I am not of Adam, nor of Eve, nor of Eden or Eden's angels.
My place is the Placeless, my trace is the Traceless;
'Tis neither body nor soul, for I belong to the soul of the Beloved.
I have put duality away, I have seen that the two worlds are one;
One I seek, One I know, One I see, One I call.
He is the first, he is the last, he is the outward, he is the inward;
I know none other except "O he" and "O he who is."
I am intoxicated with Love's cup, the worlds have passed out of my
    ken;
I have no business save mind's carouse and wild revelry.
If once in my life I spent a moment without thee,
From that time and that hour I repent of my life.
If once in this world I win a moment with thee,
I will trample on both worlds, I will dance in triumph forever.

TEVEKKUL-BEG

FROM HIS NARRATIVE CONCERNING HIS MYSTIC NOVITIATE TO
MOLLA-SHAH, WHO DIED IN 1071H-1660/61 C.E.

During an entire night he [the master] concentrated his mind on
me, while I directed my contemplation to my own heart; but the
knot of my heart would not loosen. Three nights passed in this
way, while he made me the object of his spiritual attention, yet to
no apparent effect. In the fourth night Molla-Shah said, "Tonight
Molla-Senghin and Salih-Beg, who are both very receptive to ecstatic stimulation, will concentrate their whole mind upon this
neophyte." They obeyed this command, while I remained seated,
facing Mecca, through the entire night, concentrating all my soul's
faculties upon my own heart. Toward dawn a little light and clarity
appeared in my heart, but I could distinguish neither color nor
form.

After the morning prayer I took myself, with the aforesaid two
persons, to the master, who greeted me and asked them what they
had made of me. They answered, "Ask him yourself." Upon my
telling him that I had perceived a gleam in my heart, the sheikh
became more animated and said to me, "Your heart encloses an
infinitude of colors, but it has become so dark that the gazes of
these two crocodiles of the infinite ocean [of mystical knowledge]
have not been able to restore its brightness. The moment has
come when I myself will show how to enlighten it." After these
words he bade me sit opposite him, which I did, my senses being
as if intoxicated; then he commanded me to create his own image
within myself; finally, having blindfolded my eyes, he instructed
me to concentrate all the powers of my soul upon my heart. I
obeyed, and in that moment, by divine favor and the spiritual
assistance of the sheikh, my heart was opened. I saw that within me
was something resembling an overturned cup; when this object
was stood upright, a feeling of limitless happiness filled my being.
I said to the master, "Of this cell in which I am sitting before you
I see a faithful image within me, and it appears to me as if another
Tevekkul-Beg were sitting before another Molla-Shah."

He answered, "That is good; the first apparition that meets
your eye is the image of your master; your companions [the other

novices] were prevented from this by other mystic exercises; but as for me, it is not the first time that this case presents itself to me."

He then commanded me to uncover my eyes, which I did, and I saw him sitting before me with the physical organs of sight; he had me blindfolded again, and with my mental sight I saw him sitting before me in exactly the same manner. Filled with astonishment, I exclaimed, "O Master, whether I look through my physical organs or my mental sight, always it is you I see!"

I followed the prescriptions of my master to the letter, and from day to day the spiritual world unveiled itself to me more and more; the next day I saw the forms of the prophet and his chief companions, and legions of angels and saints passed before my inner sight. Three months passed in this way; then the sphere in which all color dissolves was opened to me, and all images disappeared. During this time the master did not cease to expound to me the doctrine of union with God and mystical sight; but the absolute reality still would not reveal itself to me. The knowledge of absolute reality in relation to the comprehension of my own existence came to me only after a year's time. In that moment the following verses were revealed to my heart, from which they passed, as it were without my knowledge, to my lips:

I knew not that this corpse was anything other than water and earth;
I know not the powers of the heart, of the soul, of the body.
What misfortune that without you this time of my life passed away!
You were I, and I knew it not.

The Sufis and Their Followers

RABI'A (eighth century)

In the middle of the night she would often go up on the roof and call, "O my God! Now the tumult of day is silent, the voices are silent, and in the secret chamber the girl rejoices in her lover; but I, the lonely one, rejoice in your presence, for you are the one I acknowledge as my true lover!"

Once Rabi'a made a pilgrimage to Mecca. When she saw the Kaaba, which she had come to venerate, she said, "I need the lord of the Kaaba; what good is the Kaaba to me? I have come so close to him that his saying 'Whoever draws closer to me by an inch, I draw closer to him by a yard' applies to me. What have I to do with the Kaaba?"

When Hassan Basri admonished her to marry, she said, "My being is long since bound in matrimony. That is why I say that my being is extinguished in me and has revived in him [God]. And since that time I live in his power; indeed I am nothing but he. Whoever would have me for a bride must ask not my consent, but his." Hassan asked her how she had raised herself to this level. She said, "By losing in him all that I had found." When he inquired further, "By what method did you come to know him?" she answered, "Oh, Hassan! You know by a certain method, but I know without method."

She said, "I am consumed by an inner wound of my heart, which can only be healed through union with my friend. I shall remain sick until I achieve my goal on the Judgment Day."

Rabi'a said to God, "I keep my heart for intimacy with you, and let my body associate with those who desire my company. Thus my body is the companion of my visitor, but my well-beloved is the companion of my heart."

Neoplatonism

PLOTINUS (204–269)

Often when I awaken from the body to myself and step from otherness into myself, I behold a most wondrous beauty. It is then that I believe most strongly in my belonging to a higher destiny, and in my strength enact the perfect life, and have become One Thing with the Divine, and since I am founded in that, I attain that might and soar above all that is knowable. When, having stood thus in the Divine, I descend from spirit into thought, then I do not know how it can be that I am descending now, nor how it could be that the soul once got into my body, considering what the soul is in itself, as it has now revealed itself to me even though I am in the body.

Whosoever has seen it knows what I say: that the soul receives another life when it approaches and has already approached and has already received it; that is, when the soul experiences and comes to know this: He who leads forth the chorus of the other life is present, and now no other thing is needful, nay, all other things must be put aside, and in this One shall I stand and this One shall I become when I have cast off all veils of the extraneous. Therefore we must hasten to get out and become impatient with our bondage, so that we may embrace God with all our being and so that there may be no part of us with which we do not touch God. Then we may gaze on him here, and on ourselves too, in the manner of gazing that does good: ourselves in glory, full of spiritual light, nay, ourselves *as* pure light, unencumbered, weightless, having become God, nay, *being* God. Enkindled we are there, yet we sink down again, as if extinguished.

But why do we not remain there? Because we have not yet wholly detached ourselves. But there will be a time when we shall behold constantly, without experiencing any restlessness of the body. Yet the restlessness is not of that which gazes, but of the other: when that which gazes dismisses reflection, but does not dismiss knowl-

edge, which dwells in proofs and opinions and in the soul's thinking; but the gazing and that which gazes are no longer thought, but
greater than thought and above thought, as is that which is gazed
upon. But whoever has gazed upon himself will behold, when he
gazes, one who has become simple, or rather he will be together
with himself as such a one and will perceive himself as such a one.
That which is beheld, however—if indeed it is right to speak of the
beholder and the beheld as two instead of one, though that would
truly be a bold manner of speaking—that which is beheld is not
then seen by the beholder, nor does he distinguish and perceive
duality, but rather he has become, as it were, another and is no
longer himself and no longer belongs to himself: He belongs to
That and has become one with That, as if their centers coincide,
just as even here things that coincide are one, and only when taken
apart are they two. Thus we, too, speak now of a difference. That
is why gazing cannot be expressed. For how should one proclaim
as something different that which he saw, when he gazed upon it,
not as something different, but as One with himself?

This is evidently what is meant in the mysteries by the prohibi-
tion against communicating anything to the uninitiated. For since
That is not sayable, the Divine forbade the telling of it to those who
are not privileged to gaze upon it themselves.

Therefore since the gazer and the gazed upon were not two, but
one, just as if it were not contemplation but union, so he who was
mingled with That into One may well, upon recollection, retain an
image of That in himself. But at that time he himself was One and
had in himself no separation, nothing of himself and nothing of
others, for nothing moved in him: neither anger nor desire for
something other was in him when he ascended, nor was there any
thought or any recognition, and indeed he was wholly not himself,
if one may say even this; for he stood, transported and inspired,
in solitary calm and changeless constancy, not deviating with his
being in any direction and no longer revolving about himself, but
altogether stationary and turned to stillness. He no longer belongs
even to the Beautiful, for he has left even the Beautiful beneath
him; he has paced beyond the round dance of the virtues, like one
entered into the inner sanctum, and left the statues of the gods
behind him in the temple; they do not meet his eye again until he
leaves the inner sanctum, where he has gazed upon and united

with that which is not image and form, but himself; now these become a secondary sight for him. However, it was no gazing, but another way of becoming aware, a stepping out and a becoming simple and a calm and a meditation on union: if one really beholds That-which-is, in the inner sanctum.

Gnosticism and Early Christian Heresy

VALENTINUS (SECOND CENTURY)

Valentinus says that he once saw a newborn babe and inquired of it, saying, "Who art thou?" The child answered, saying: "I am the Logos." Then Valentinus added a tragic myth. . . .

BEGINNING OF THE MYTH

> I see in my mind how all is suspended.
> I see in my mind how all is supported.
> I see the flesh suspended from the soul,
> the soul supported by the air,
> the air suspended from the ether,
> from the abyss fruits have sprung forth,
> from the mother's womb a child has sprung forth.

SAYINGS OF MONTANUS AND HIS FEMALE DISCIPLES (SECOND CENTURY)

Montanus: "The Paraclete says, 'Behold, the human being is like a lyre, and I light upon the strings like a plectrum. The human being sleeps, and I am awake. Behold, it is the Lord who takes the human heart out of the breast and gives the human being a heart.' "

Prisca: "Purity unites them, and they see visions, and bending down their faces they hear distinct voices, both healing ones and hidden ones."

Maximilla: (the Spirit speaking through her): "I am pursued like a wolf among sheep; I am no wolf; I am word and spirit and strength."

Greek Monasticism

SYMEON THE NEW THEOLOGIAN (ca. 970–1040)

FROM THE "LOVE SONGS TO GOD"

Come, O thou whom my poor soul has desired and desires. Come, lonely one, to the lonely, for lonely I am, as thou seest. Come, thou who has made me isolated and solitary in this world. Come, thou who hast become my desire, who has made me to desire thee, whom none may reach by striving. Come, my breath and my life. Come, jubilation and glory and my constant delight. I give thee thanks that thou has become one spirit with me without mingling, transformation, or exchange; and that thou who art God over all has become all in all to me. Unexplainable sustenance, impossible to consume, that pours perpetually through the lips of my soul and fills to overflowing the fountain of my heart. Flashing raiment, which scorches the demons. Affliction which purifies me through the unceasing and holy tears which thy presence gives to those to whom thou comest.

   I give thee thanks because thou hast become for me a day without evening and a sun without sunset: thou that hast no place in which to hide thyself, seeing that thou fillest the world with thy glory. Never has thou hidden thyself from anyone, but it is we who hide ourselves from thee, because we do not want to come to thee. For where shouldst thou hide thyself, since thou hast nowhere a place in which to rest? Or why shouldst thou hide thyself, since there is not one of all whom thou dost despise or shun? Then, Lord of Love, do thou pitch a tent in me and dwell in me, and until my passing away separate thyself not and sunder thyself not from me, thy servant, so that in my death and after my death I too may find myself in thee and rule with thee, God, who art Lord of all. Remain, Lord, and do not leave me alone, so that when my enemies come, who seek constantly to devour my flesh, they may behold thee dwelling in me and flee far and farther away and not

have the victory over me, when they see thee, who art stronger
than all, resting within the dwelling of my humble soul. In truth,
just as thou didst remember, O Lord, that I was in the world, and
didst without my knowledge elect and elevate me out of the world
and place me before the countenance of thy glory, do thou make
me firm within, unmoved forevermore, and protect me through
thy dwelling in me, so that in gazing upon thee daily I the dead may
live, in possessing thee I the poor may be rich. So shall I be
mightier than all kings; and eating and drinking thee and wrapping
myself in thee at particular hours I shall enjoy unspeakable bliss.

My tongue lacks words, and what is occurring in me my mind
sees, but does not interpret. It contemplates and would utter, but
it does not find the words. It sees the invisible, that which is bare
of all form, altogether simple, not composed of parts, and infinite
in greatness. For it sees no beginning, and beholds no end, and
is conscious of no center at all, and knows not how it shall say what
it sees. Something whole is appearing, as I believe, and not with
its own being, but through participation. For you may light a fire
from fire, and you receive the whole fire, yet the fire remains
undiminished and undivided as before. Nevertheless what is trans-
mitted separates itself from the first, and as something physical it
goes into several lights. But this is something spiritual, immeasurable, inseparable, and inexhaustible. For in giving itself it does not
divide into many, but remains undivided, and is in me, and breaks
forth in my poor heart like a sun or the round disk of the sun, like
the light, for it is a light. I do not know what to say of it. And I
would be silent—would that I could—but the miracle, full of awe,
stirs up the soul and pries open my unclean mouth; and he who
awakened the sunrise in my dark heart now forces me, unwilling,
to speak and to write.

What is, O my savior, this thy measureless mercy? How hast thou
deigned to make me, the unclean, the lost, the wanton, into a limb
of thy body? How hast thou arrayed me in the brightest raiment,
which flashes with the splendor of immortality and makes all my
limbs bright? For thy whole, immaculate, divine body, unmingled,
and yet mingled in some inexpressible way, flashes in the fire of
thy divinity, and this hast thou given me, my God. For thy most
immaculate body unites with this my filthy and perishable hovel,
and my blood mixes with thy blood. I know that I am also joined

to thy divinity and have become thy body most pure, a shining limb, a limb truly holy that gleams far and wide. I gaze upon beauty, I gaze upon splendor, I behold the light of thy mercy and stare into the inexplicable lightning, and am beside myself when I note what I have been and what—O wonder—I have become: And I revere and dread myself, honor and fear myself as I honor and fear thee, and am bewildered and dismayed; for I know not where I shall sit and whom I may approach and on what I shall lean your limbs, and for what works, what deeds, I am to use such sacred and divine limbs.

I am loved by him who is not in this world. And amid this cell I see him who is outside the world. I sit upon my bed, and abide outside the world. Yet I see him who is eternal and yet born, and speak with him and dare to say: I love, for he loves me. I feed on contemplation; I clothe myself in it; united with him I transcend the heavens. And that all this is true and certain, I know. But where this body is then, of that I have no cognizance. I know that he who is unmoved descends. I know that he who is by nature such that no eye may gaze upon him is gazed upon by me. I know that he who is far removed from every creature takes me up in himself and hides me in his arms, and I find myself outside the whole world. And then again, I who am mortal and an insignificant person in the world, behold the entire Creator of the world in myself; and even while I live, I embrace all blossoming life in myself and know that I shall not die. In my heart he is, and dwells in heaven: Here and there I see him in the same radiance.

We are limbs of Christ; Christ is our limb. And my hand, the hand of the poorest creature, is Christ; and my foot is Christ; and I, the poorest creature, am the hand and foot of Christ. I move my hand, and so does Christ, for he, in entirety, is my hand: You must understand that the Godhead is undivided. I move my foot—it shines as he does. Say not that I blaspheme, but confirm this and adore Christ, who has made you so. For you too, if you will, can become his limb. And so all the limbs of each of us will become limbs of Christ and Christ will become our limb, and he will make all that is ugly and ill-formed beautiful and well-formed, adorning it with the splendor and dignity of his divinity; and we shall all together become gods, intimately united with God, aware of no blemish on our bodies, but sharing fully in the resemblance to the entire body of Christ; so each of us shall have all of Christ. For the One, when he has become many, remains One undivided; but every part is the whole Christ.

He himself is present and shines in my poor heart, clothes me in immortal splendor and shines through all my limbs, embraces me wholly, kisses me wholly, and gives himself entirely to me, unworthy as I am; and I take my fill of his love and beauty and am filled with the rapture and sweetness of the Godhead. I receive a share in the light, a share in the glory, and my countenance shines like that of him who is my desire, and all my limbs become bright; I become more splendid than the splendid, richer than the rich, mightier than all the wielders of might; and I am greater than kings, and far more honored than all visible things, not only the earth and what is on earth, but even heaven and what is in the heavens, since I have with me the shaper of all things, to whom belongs the praise and the honor now and eternally. Amen.

When he had filled me with heavenly joy, he flew away and took my spirit, my mind and my desire for all earthly things with him. And following him, my spirit demanded to embrace the splendor I had beheld, but did not find him as creature, and did not succeed in going out from among the creatures, that it might embrace that uncreated and uncomprehended splendor. Nevertheless it went about everywhere and strove to see him. It explored the air; it walked all around the heavens; it crossed the abysses; it spied out, so it thought, the ends of the world. But in all this it found nothing, for all was created. And I lamented and sorrowed and burned in my core and lived like one removed in spirit. But he came at his own will and, descending like a bright cloud of mist, seemed to surround my head entirely, so that I cried out in consternation. But he, flying off again, left me alone. And when I laboriously sought him I suddenly came to know that he was in myself, and in the center of my heart he appeared like the light of a sun, round as a circle. When he had revealed himself thus, and I had recognized and received him, he put the whirlwind of demons to flight, repulsed my cowardly dread, put strength into me, stripped my soul of earthly thoughts and reclothed me with the thoughts of the spirit. From the things that are seen he severed me, and with those that are not seen he connected me. He permitted me to see the uncreated and to rejoice that I have been sundered from the created, from the visible, from that which swiftly passes away, and am united with the uncreated, the immortal, which has no beginning and cannot be seen by anyone. Such is mercy.

Leave me alone, locked in my cell. Let me go with God, who alone is kind. Step back, go away. Let me die alone in the sight of God, who formed me. Let none knock on the door. Let none raise his voice. Let none of my relatives and friends visit me. Let no one distract my mind from the contemplation of the good and beautiful Lord. Let no one hand me food; let no one bring me drink. For it is enough for me to die in the sight of my God, the good, merciful God, who descended to earth in order to call the sinners and to lead them with him into the heavenly life. I no longer wish to gaze on the light of this world, nor the sun itself, nor anything that is in this world. For I see my Lord, I see the King. I see the light that truly is and the creator of all light. I see the source of all beauty. I see the cause of all things. I see the beginning that has no beginning, by which everything was brought forth and by which everything lives and receives nourishment, and from whose will everything passes away and ceases to be. When I gazed upon him, I lost my senses. You, therefore, whom the senses command, let me depart and permit me to lock myself in my cell and to sit in there; and when I hide myself there as in a pit and live a life outside the whole world, gazing upon my immortal Lord and creator, I shall want to die of his love, yet shall know that I shall not die at all.

You whom the common cannot comprehend, how in my hands you become truly small, and shining you bend toward my lips like an udder of light and a sweetness, O of mystery. And now give yourself to me, that I may take my fill of you, that I may kiss and embrace your unspeakable glory, the light of your countenance, and be fulfilled and impart to all others and, in solitude, enter into you entirely glorified. From your light may I myself become light, that I may stand by you and, relieved of the cares of many evils, may be freed from the fear that I may again be changed to what I was. Give me this too, Lord, grant me this too, you who have given everything else to me, unworthy as I am. This is what I most need, and in this is everything. For although even now you suffer me to gaze on you, although you have mercy on me, although even now you enlighten and mystically teach me and watch over me and protect me with your mighty hand and stand by me, and put the demons to flight and annihilate them, and make everything subject to me, and proffer everything to me, and fill me with all that is good —my God, still I gain nothing by all this unless you grant that without shame I may pass through the gates of death; unless the Prince of Darkness, approaching, sees your glory beside me and is confounded, the dark one consumed by your inaccessible light, and with him all hostile powers behold the sign of the seal and turn to flee from it, but I, trusting in your mercy, stride resolutely across, approach you and fall down before you. What fruit shall I receive of that which occurs in me now? None, truly; rather it will inflame still more the fire that is in me.

Once again I saw him wholly within my house, and amid these furnishings he arose unexpectedly and united himself to me in an inexpressible manner, bound himself to me ineffably and united himself to me without mixture as fire to iron or light to glass. And he made me like unto fire and light. And I became that which I formerly saw and beheld from afar. I do not know how to report to you the wonderful manner of this. For I could not discern, and even now do not discern at all, how he entered into me and united with me. But being united with him, how shall I tell you who he is who has united with me, and with whom I have united? I fear that if I say it you will not believe it, and that falling from ignorance into blasphemy you, my brother, may lose your soul. I and he with whom I am united have become one. But how shall I call myself, who have been united with him? God, dual by nature, one in being, makes me also double and, as you see, has implanted in me too a double name. This is the distinction: I am human by nature; by grace I am God.

Again the light blazes for me. Again I see the light clearly. Again it opens the skies; again it drives away the night. Again it reveals everything. Again it alone is seen. Again it leads me away from everything visible, from all things that belong to the senses, it tears me away from them. And he who is above all the heavens, whom no human has ever seen, he comes again into my spirit, without leaving heaven, without cleaving the night, without dividing the air, without breaking through the roof of the house, without penetrating any thing, and into the middle of my heart, O lofty mystery, where everything remains as it is, the light plunges and uplifts me over everything. And I, who was amid all things, stand outside all, I do not know, perhaps even outside the body. Now I am in truth altogether there where the light is alone and simple, and from the contemplation of it I emerge simply in purity.

The Twelfth Century

HILDEGARD VON BINGEN (1099–1179)

FROM A LETTER

O faithful servant, I, a poor female form, speak these words to you in the true vision. If it should please God to elevate my body in this vision, as he elevates the soul, still the fear would not depart from my spirit and my heart, for I know that I am a human being, who has since childhood been enclosed [within the silence of this vision]. Many wise men have become so confused by miracles that they indeed revealed many a secret, but for the sake of vain renown ascribed it to themselves, and so they fell. But those who in the ascent of the soul drew their wisdom from God and counted themselves as nothing, have become the pillars of heaven. . . .

And how should this be, if I, poor wretch, did not know myself? God works in the way he chooses, for the glory of his name and not of the earthly human. But I have always a trembling fear, for I have no assurance in myself concerning any possibility; rather I stretch out my hands to God, so that I am borne by him like a feather, which has none of the heaviness of strength and which flies in the wind that carries it. And what I behold I cannot know perfectly, as long as I am in this bodily office and in the invisible soul; for in these two states the human being is defective.

But from my childhood, since before I grew strong in bones and nerves and veins, I have constantly beheld this vision in my soul until the present time, when I am more than seventy years old. And my soul ascends in this vision, as God wills, to the height of the firmament and into the exchange of various airs and extends itself to many different peoples who live far from me in distant lands and spaces. And when I see this in such manner in my soul, I also perceive it according to the changes of the layer of clouds and other created things. Yet I do not hear it with the outward ears, nor receive it in the thoughts of my heart, nor with any contribution of my five senses, but rather in my soul alone, while my outward eyes are open, so that I never suffer in them the weariness of ecstasy, but gaze upon it waking by day and in the night. And I am constantly oppressed by illnesses and am often so involved in severe pains that they threaten to bring me death; but God has sustained me up till this time.

The light I see is not local; it is far, far brighter than the cloud that carries the sun. And I cannot see depth or length or breadth in it. And it is called for me that shadow of the living light. And as sun, moon, and stars are reflected in the water, so in this light the images of the writings and the speech and the forces and many works of men shine forth to me.

But whatever I see or experience in this vision, I remember for a long time, so that I can recall when I have seen and heard it. And at the same time I see it and hear it and know it, and what I see I possess at the moment. But what I do not see I do not know, for I am without learning and have only been taught to read the letters in simple fashion. And what I write in the vision, I see and hear, and I set down no other words than those I hear, and in unpolished language I bring them forth, just as I hear them in the vision. For in this vision I am not taught to write as the philosophers write. And the words in this vision are not like the words that sound from the mouths of human beings, but like a vibrating flame and like a cloud moving in pure air.

I can by no means make out the form of this light, just as I cannot completely gaze at the sun's disk. In this light, however, I some-times and not often see another light, which is called for me the living light, and when and in what manner I see this, I do not know how to say. And when I gaze on it, all sadness and all need are snatched away from me, so that I then have the manners of a simple little girl and not those of an old woman.

But because of the constant weakness I suffer, I am reluctant to utter all the words and visions that have been shown to me. But in the time when my soul gazes on them and enjoys them, I am brought into such a different state of mind that, as I say, I consign all woe and pain to oblivion. And what I see and hear in that vision, my soul draws up as from a spring that still remains full and unexhausted. But at no time is my soul bereft of the light that is called the shadow of the living light. And I see it as I see in a bright cloud the firmament without stars. And therein I see what I often speak and what I answer when I am asked about the lightning flashes of that living light.

ALPAIS OF CUDOT (1150–1211)

When a pious man asked her whether she saw her visions in the body or outside the body, and whether she had ever been entranced in spirit, she answered:

"Whether I have been or was entranced, I dare not say, nor have I an opinion, just as I do not dare to claim, touching these visions which I report at your urging, that it happened or is happening in the reality of things as it was shown to me in my repose as happening; rather it is safer for me to leave that to the divine judgment, from which nothing is hidden. But the visions I report to you I see in my repose as happening in the manner I report them. But what they refer to or what they mean or what most of them want and whether they have occurred and been established in the manner and order in which they appear to me to have occurred and been established, this I do not know well. But however the truth of this thing may be, this one thing I know, that I am not deceived or deceiving; for what I say, I see as I say it, and I say it as I see it. But whether I see what the Lord is pleased to show me when he rests in me or my spirit in him, in the body or out of the body, I do not know. He alone knows it who knows everything and who gives me sight, sometimes waking and sometimes in sleep, or rather in repose.

"But once it appeared to me—if I may say it, although I dare not assert it as certain—that I had been outside the body. But how and when my soul left its body, how it threw off the body, I cannot tell. For so lightly and suddenly, in an instant, as it seemed to me, did my soul throw off the cloak of flesh, as when one clad in an open cloak is running along the road, and the cloak slips suddenly from the shoulders of the runner, who is entirely given over to the eagerness of his path and his running, and it falls to the ground without his knowing anything of it; he notices that it has fallen only when he sees himself naked and his cloak lying beneath him on the ground. Thus, as it seems to me, my soul suddenly left my body, quite without my knowledge. I perceived it only when my soul, stripped of its flesh, began to contemplate its body, which lay motionless upon the bed. It looked at the body and rejoiced in gazing and delighted in it, for it appeared very beautiful to her, it was precious in her sight, and she felt of it and lifted it up. And very heavy and burdensome was its weight to my soul, still my soul loved it and embraced it with wondrous passion.

"While my soul was thus gazing upon the body from outside, she looked around and saw an endless crowd of people running hither and thither like wild beasts, as if raving and out of their senses, as if they wanted to flee but could not find the path of flight. At the hubbub they made, my soul took fright and began to tremble, and quicker than a word she entered the body again, but I had no idea how and when she returned into it. For as I neither knew nor felt in what manner she left the body and threw it off, so I neither felt nor found in what manner she returned home to it. Like someone asleep in a boat which, flying softly over the water, has already reached the harbor, but he does not know or understand in what manner he has come to shore."

When asked what sort of thing the soul was and whether the soul could see itself as well as the body it had left, and what kind of eyes it had to see itself or the body, she replied that she could not explain this clearly, for in the whole world no object could be found, according to whose image and form the nature of the soul could be set forth.

"For the soul," she said, "is simple, invisible, and incorporeal; is not divided into parts like the body, nor into limbs, for it has no hands or feet with which it could walk or feel, no eyes or ears with which it could see or hear. For in all its actions and movements it is wholly present. Whatever it touches, it touches as a whole and all at once, and all at once it experiences and apprehends soft or hard; warm and cold it distinguishes with the fingertip as a whole; what it smells, it smells as a whole and absorbs fragrances with all its being; what it tastes, it tastes as a whole, and as a whole distinguishes each taste; what it hears, it hears as a whole and as a whole recalls the sounds; what it sees, it sees as a whole and as a whole remembers the images. In short, the soul feels, smells, tastes, hears, sees, and remembers as a whole.

"And thus it also sees itself when it is released from the flesh. For as long as it is in the flesh it cannot see itself as a whole, because it cannot gather itself wholly into itself in order to see itself alone: Ideas and images of bodily things occur to it, which it receives through the outward senses of the body and by which it is prevented from seeing itself whole. The soul is not fixed in a single place, for it is not local; it is not limited by any space, for it has no extension; it is not confined by any limbs, for it is incorporeal. It is not detained by the size of the place, so as to occupy a larger space with a larger part, or a smaller space with a smaller part, or so that in one part there would be less of it than in the whole. For in every little part of the body it is present all at once. Therefore at whatsoever place a part of the body, however small, is struck or pierced, the whole soul feels the pain. And the soul is not lesser in the smaller parts of the body, or greater in the larger parts; rather in some of them it blooms more strongly, in others more weakly, but in the smallest it is whole, in the greatest it is whole, in all it is whole, and in the single part it is whole.

"For as God is everywhere, God is whole in his whole world and whole in each of his creatures, animating, moving, and governing all; as the apostle says that in him we live and move and have our being, in like manner the soul is strong everywhere in the body, as it were in its world, and animates, moves, and governs it—more strongly, no doubt, in the heart and brain, just as God is said to be in heaven in a particular way. And just as he is within and without in his world, and above and below, so the soul is in its body, governing it from above, supporting it from below, filling it from within, encompassing it from without. Thus it is within as well as without, it encompasses as well as penetrates, it both leads and supports; and as God neither grows with the growth of the creatures nor wastes away in their decline, so the soul is not lessened with the lessening of its members, nor increased by their increase."

The Franciscans

FROM 1208, AEGIDIUS WAS A DISCIPLE OF ST. FRANCIS

In the sixth year after his conversion, when he was living in the monastery at Fabriano, the hand of the Lord came upon him one night. While he was fervently praying, he was filled with such great comfort from God that it seemed to him that God wanted to lead his soul out of the body that he might gaze upon God's mysteries in clarity. And he began to feel his body becoming lifeless, first in the feet and then further, until the soul left it. And while standing outside the body, as it seemed to him, by the will of him who had bound the soul to the body, his soul delighted in the surpassing beauty wherewith the Holy Spirit had adorned it, and in the contemplation of itself. For it was very delicate and very bright beyond all measure, as he himself related before his death. Then this very holy soul was led away to the contemplation of heavenly mysteries, which he would never reveal.

Once he said, "I know a man who saw God so clearly that he lost all faith."

Another time Brother Andreas said to him, "You say that in a vision God took away your faith; tell me, if it please you, whether you have hope."

He answered, "He who has no faith, how should he have hope?"

Brother Andreas said to him, "Do you not hope to possess eternal life?"

Brother Aegidius answered, "Do you not believe that God, if it please him, can give a pledge of eternal life?"

Brother Aegidius said that he had been born four times. "The first time," he said, "I was born of my physical mother, the second time in the sacrament of baptism, the third time when I entered this holy order, the fourth time when God granted me the grace of his appearance."

Then Brother Andreas said to him, "If I should go into distant lands and someone asked me whether I knew you and how you fared, I could answer thus: "It is thirty-two years since Brother Aegidius was born, and before he was born he had faith, but after his birth he lost his faith.' "

Brother Aegidius answered, "As you have said, so it is. True, before then I did not have faith as perfectly as I should have had it; nevertheless God took it from me. But even from him who has it in a perfect manner, the way one should have it, God will take it away. After that I did such things that I deserve to have a rope tied around my neck and be dragged in shame through all the streets of the city."

Again Brother Andreas said, "If you do not have faith, what would you do if you were a priest and had to celebrate High Mass? How could you say, 'I believe in one God'? It seems that you would have to say, 'I know one God.' "

Then Brother Aegidius answered with a very joyous countenance and sang in a loud voice, "I know one God, the Almighty Father."

When Saint Louis, the king of France, decided to make a pilgrimage to the holy places and heard of Brother Aegidius's reputation for holiness, he resolved in his heart to visit him. When in the course of his wanderings he came for that purpose to Perugia, where he had heard that Brother Aegidius was staying, he went to the gate of the brothers like a poor unknown pilgrim, accompanied only by a few companions, and asked urgently to see Brother Aegidius. The porter went and told Brother Aegidius that a pilgrim at the gate desired to see him. Immediately he knew through the spirit who it was. And stepping out of his cell as if drunken, he came running to the gate, and both of them fell into a wondrous embrace and, kneeling, gave each other kisses of great devotion, as if they had been friends from ancient times. When they had given each other the signs of fervent love, neither spoke a word to the other, but they parted, each one keeping silence in his own way.

After Saint Louis had gone his way, the brothers asked one of his companions who it was that Brother Aegidius had embraced so fervently. He answered that it was Louis, the king of France, who was on a pilgrimage and had wished to see the holy Brother Aegidius. Then the brothers complained to Brother Aegidius, saying, "O Brother Aegidius, why did you not want to say anything to so great a king, who came from France in order to see you and to hear a good word from you?"

Answered Aegidius, "Dearest brothers, do not be surprised that he could say nothing to me, nor I to him; for the moment we embraced, the light of divine wisdom revealed his heart to me and mine to him. And standing in the eternal mirror we learned with complete comfort what he had intended to say to me and I to him, without noises of the lips and the tongue, and better than if we had spoken with the lips. And had we attempted to explain in vocal sounds what we felt within, such speech would have brought us sorrow rather than comfort. Know, then, that wondrously comforted he departed hence."

The Thirteenth and Fourteenth Centuries in Germany

MECHTILD VON MAGDEBURG (1217–1277)

OF THE SOUL'S PRESENTATION AT COURT, IN WHICH GOD SHOWS HIMSELF

When the poor soul comes to court she is wise and well-behaved; she gazes merrily upon her Creator. O how joyfully she is received then. Then she is silent and desires his praise immeasurably. Then he shows her, with great desire, his divine heart. It is like red-gold that burns in a great fire of coals. Then he puts the soul into his glowing heart, so that the lofty prince and the little girl embrace and are united like water and wine. Then she is annihilated and is beside herself, so that she is altogether helpless. And he is sick with love for her, as he was from the beginning, for nothing can be either added to him or taken away from him. Then she says, "Lord, you are my comfort, my desire, my flowing spring, my sun, and I am your mirror." This is the presentation at court of the loving soul, who cannot be without God.

HOW THE SOUL RECEIVES GOD AND GIVES PRAISE

O joyful sight! O friendly greeting! O fond embrace! Lord, the wonder of you has wounded me, your grace has overpowered me. O you high cliff, you are so hidden that none can nest in you save doves and nightingales.

HOW GOD RECEIVES THE SOUL

Welcome, dear dove, you have flown so much in the earthly kingdom that your wings have grown strong enough for the heavenly kingdom.

GOD COMPARES THE SOUL TO FOUR THINGS

You taste like the grape; you are fragrant as balsam; you shine like the sun; you are an addition to my highest love.

THE SOUL PRAISES GOD IN FIVE THINGS

O you pouring God in your giving! O you flowing God in your love! O you burning God in your desire! O you melting God in the union with your beloved! O you resting God on my breasts, without whom I cannot be!

GOD SPEAKS ENDEARMENTS TO THE SOUL IN SIX THINGS

You are the pillow for my head, my bed of delight, my most secret rest, my deepest desire, my highest honor. You are a pleasure of my divinity, a consolation of my humanity, a brook for my torch.

THE SOUL RETURNS GOD'S PRAISE IN SIX THINGS

You are my mountain of glass, the feast of my eyes, the loss of my self, the storm of my heart, the dissolution and ruin of my nature, my highest security.

OF KNOWLEDGE AND ENJOYMENT

To the wise soul love without knowledge seems like darkness, knowledge without love like a hellish torment. Enjoyment without dying fills her with inconsolable grief.

OF THE MESSAGE TO SAINT MARY

The sweet dew of the Trinity without beginning has leaped from the spring of the eternal Godhead into the womb of the chosen maiden, and the fruit of the womb is an immortal God and a mortal man and a living consolation of eternal joy, and our salvation has become a bridegroom. The bride is intoxicated with gazing on the noble face. In the greatest strength she comes out of herself, and in the greatest blindness she sees with the greatest clarity. In the greatest clarity she is dead and alive at the same time. The longer she is dead, the more merrily she lives. The more merrily she lives, the more she learns. The smaller she becomes, the more abundance she receives. The richer she becomes, the poorer she is. The deeper she dwells, the broader she is. The more imperious she is, the deeper her wounds become. The higher she soars, the nearer she comes to the Godhead, the more beautifully she shines with the reflection of the Godhead. The more she works, the more softly she rests. The more she comprehends, the stiller her silence. The louder she calls, the greater the miracles that she works with her power according to her ability.

The more his desire grows, the more tightly he holds her, and the greater is the happiness of the bride. The more fervent the embrace, the sweeter the taste of the kisses. The more lovingly they gaze at each other, the harder it is for them to part. The more he gives her, the more she consumes, however much she has. The more humbly she says farewell, the sooner she returns. The hotter she remains, the sooner does her flame die down. The more she burns, the more beautifully she shines. The more God's praise is spread abroad, the less her hunger dwindles.

Ah, whither is our Savior-bridegroom being conveyed in the jubilation of the holy Trinity? Since God no longer wanted to be in himself, he made the soul and gave himself to her out of great love. Of what are you made, soul, that you rise so high over all creatures, and mingle with the holy Trinity and yet remain wholly in yourself?—You have spoken of my origin, now I tell it to you truly: I was made in that place from love, therefore no creature can satisfy me according to my noble nature, and no creature can unlock me, except love alone.

YOU SHALL ASK GOD TO LOVE YOU MIGHTILY, OFTEN, AND LONG, THAT YOU MAY BE PURE, BEAUTIFUL, AND HOLY

O Lord, love me mightily and love me often and long; the oftener you love me, the purer I become; the more mightily you love me, the more beautiful I become; the longer you love me, the holier I become here on earth.

HOW GOD ANSWERS THE SOUL

That I love you often, that I have from my nature, for I myself am love. That I love you mightily, that comes from my desire, for I too desire to be loved mightily. That I love you long, that comes from my eternity, for I am without end.

GOD ASKS THE SOUL WHAT SHE IS BRINGING

God speaks: "You hunt a great deal in love. Tell me, what are you bringing me, my queen?"

The soul: Lord, I bring you my jewel: It is greater than the mountains, wider than the world, deeper than the sea, higher than the clouds, brighter than the sun, more manifold than the stones; it weighs more than the whole earth."

God: "O you image of my divinity, exalted with my humanity, adorned with my holy spirit, what is the name of your jewel?"

The soul: "Lord, its name is my heart's desire, which I have withdrawn from the world, kept for myself and denied to all creatures, only I can carry it no longer. Lord, where shall I lay it down?"

God: "You shall lay down your heart's desire nowhere save in my divine heart and on my human breast. Only there will you be consoled and kissed with my spirit."

OF THE WAY OF LOVE IN SEVEN THINGS, OF THE THREE GOWNS OF THE BRIDE, AND OF THE DANCE

God: "O loving soul, would you know what your way is?"

The soul: "Yes, dear Holy Spirit, teach me."

God: "When you have gotten over the distress of repentance and the torment of confession, and the labor of penance, and the desire of the world, and the temptation of the devil, and the exuberance of the flesh, and the perverted self-will that pulls many souls backward so badly that they never again attain the true joy, and when you have struck down all your worst enemies, then you will be so tired that you say, 'Beautiful youth, I desire you, where shall I find you?' "

Then **the youth** speaks: "I hear a voice that sounds to me like love. I have wooed her for many days, but the voice was not close to me. Now I am moved, I must go toward her. It is she who bears sorrow and love at the same time. In the morning in the dew, then is the embraced devotion that first enters the soul."

Now speak her chamberlains, who are the five **senses**: "Lady, you must clothe yourself."

The soul: "Love, whither shall I go?"

The senses: "We have overheard you whispering; the prince will come toward you in the dew and in the lovely song of birds. Come then, lady, and do not tarry long."

Now she puts on a shift of the gentlest humility; so humble is it that it can suffer nothing to be beneath it. Over that a white gown of pure chastity, so pure that it can no longer suffer any thought, word, or touch that might sully it. Then she enfolds herself in the cloak of holy repute, which she has won with all virtues.

So she goes into the forest, in the company of holy people. There the sweetest nightingales of harmonious union with God sing all day and all night long, and she hears there many voices of the birds of holy knowledge. The youth has not yet arrived. Now she sends forth messengers, for she wants to dance; she sends for the faith of Abraham, the longing of the prophets, and the chaste humility of our Lady, Saint Mary, and for all the holy virtues of Jesus Christ, and all the piety of his elect. Then a beautiful dance of praise begins.

Then comes **the youth** and speaks to her: "Maiden, you should dance as piously after my chosen ones as they have danced before you."

Then **the maiden** says: "I cannot dance, Lord, unless you lead me. If you want me to skip, then you yourself must sing. Then I will dance into love, out of love into knowledge, out of knowledge into enjoyment, out of enjoyment beyond all human senses. There I will remain and yet continue to vibrate."

And so **the youth** must sing thus for the dance: "For me to you and for me out of myself, gladly with you, sad when we're parted."

Then **the youth** says: "Maiden, this dance in honor you have well performed. You shall have your way with the son of the virgin, for now you are weary in your innermost being. Come at noon to the shadowy spring, into the bed of love. There you shall cool yourself with him."

Then speaks **the maiden**: "O Lord, it is overgreat that she is thy love's mate who has in her no love save thou in her dost move."

Then **the soul** speaks to the senses, who are her chamberlains: "Now I am tired of dancing for a while. Leave me, I must go where I may find coolness."

Then **the senses** say to the soul: "Lady, if you wish to cool yourself in the love tears of Saint Mary Magdalene, it will do you good."

The soul: "Gentlemen, be silent, for you know not all that I have in mind. Let me go without hindrance. I wish to drink now from the unmixed wine."

The senses: "Lady, in the chastity of the virgins rests the great love."

The soul: "That may well be, for me it is not the highest."

The senses: "In the blood of the martyrs you could cool yourself splendidly."

The soul: "I am martyred so often that I do not want to go there now."

The senses: "In the counsel of those who profess the faith, good people are glad to dwell."

The soul: "In that counsel I will always stand with all I do and refrain from doing, but now I do not wish to go there."

The senses: "In the wisdom of the apostles you will find great security."

The soul: "I have wisdom with me here, and with it I will choose the best."

The senses: "Lady, the angels are pure, and lovely and radiant to look upon; if you wish to cool yourself, betake yourself to them."

The soul: "The joy of the angels is but grief to me, unless their Lord my bridegroom in their midst I see."

The senses: "Then cool yourself in the holy penitent's ways that John the Baptist had by God's grace."

The soul: "Torment I would not shun, but by love's power all toil is overcome."

The senses: "Lady, if you would cool yourself in love, then bend in the lap of the Virgin toward the little child, and look and see how the bliss of the angels drank the supernatural milk of the eternal Maiden."

The soul: "That is a child's delight, the suckling and rocking of a child. I am a full-grown bride; I will go to my true love's side."

The senses: "O lady, if you go there, then we must go blind altogether. For the Godhead is so fiery hot, as you yourself well know, that all the fire and all the heat that shines and burns through heaven and all the saints, all of it flowed out of his divine breath and from his human mouth, by the will of the Holy Spirit. How could you remain there even for an hour?"

The soul: "The fish in water cannot drown, nor the bird in the air sink down. Gold cannot perish in the fire where its pure shining is acquired. God has given to every creature to live according to its nature. How, then, can I resist my nature? I had to go out of all things into God, who is my father by nature, my brother by his humanity, my bridegroom by love, and I am his without beginning. Do you wish me not to find my own? He can do both, burn powerfully and cool comfortingly. But do not grieve overmuch; you will still have a chance to teach me. When I return I shall have great need of your teaching, for the earth is full of many dangers."

So then the best loved she goes to the handsomest he in the secret chamber of the pure Godhead; there she finds the bed of love and the alcove of love and God and man ready.

Then says our **God**: "Remain standing, Dame Soul."

The soul: "What is your command, Lord?"

God: "You must get undressed."

The soul: "Lord, how can that be?"

God: "Dame Soul, you are so natured in me, that nothing must come between us. There was never an angel, however high, to whom was given for an hour that which is given you for eternity. Therefore you shall put fear and shame from you and all outward virtues. You should wish to find in eternity only the virtue that you bear within yourself by nature, that is, your noble longing and your unfathomable desire. These I will fill eternally with my infinite riches."

The soul: "Lord, now I am a naked soul, and you in yourself a glorious God. Our companionship is eternal bliss without death."

And now his will and her will both are blissfully fulfilled. He gives himself to her, and she gives herself to him. What happens to her then, she knows, and I am content with that. But it cannot last long. Where two lovers are together secretly, all too often they must swiftly part.

Dear friend of God, this way of love I have described to you. May God give you this way in your heart. Amen.

A SONG OF THE SOUL TO GOD IN FIVE THINGS, AND HOW GOD IS THE GARMENT OF THE SOUL AND THE SOUL, OF GOD

You shine into my soul as the sun into gold. When I may rest in you, Lord, my bliss is surpassing great. My soul is your garment fair, and you my soul's inmost garment are. That any difference there must be is sorest grief of heart to me. If your loving were more strong, my days here would not be long, then I could love you ceaselessly; for this I long. Now I have sung to thee, 'tis not as it should be, if you would sing to me, it would go right merrily.

AN ANTIPHONY OF GOD TO THE SOUL IN FIVE THINGS

God speaks: "When I shine, you must gleam. When I flow, you must ripple. When you sigh, you draw my divine heart into you. When you weep after me, I take you into my arms. But when you love, we become one. And when we two are thus one, there can be no parting, only a blissful waiting dwells between us two."

The soul: "Lord, so I wait then with hunger and thirst, with hunting and longing, until the hour of play when your divine mouth will say the chosen words that flow for no one, and are heard by the soul alone, when out of earthly things she slips and lays her ear against your lips; the treasure of love is made known to her alone."

OF THE COMPLAINT OF THE LOVING SOUL THAT GOD SPARES HER AND WITHDRAWS HIS GIFT FROM HER. OF WISDOM, HOW THE SOUL ASKS GOD WHO HE IS AND HOW HE IS. OF THE GARDEN, OF THE FLOWERS AND THE SONG OF THE VIRGINS

The soul speaks: "O you treasure, immeasurable in your fullness! O you miracle, incomprehensibly manifold! O you infinite power in the lordship of your majesty! With what sorrow I long for you, seeing that you wish to spare me; could all earth's creatures make my moan, the tale of my woe would not be done. For I suffer sorrow measureless; to this a human death were gentleness. I seek you with my thoughts as a maiden secretly seeks her lover. I suffer violent pain, for I am bound to you. The bond is stronger than I am, so I cannot get free of love. I call you with great desire, with piteous voice. I wait for you with a heavy heart, I cannot rest, I burn inextinguishably in the heat of your love. I hunt you with all my might. But if I had the strength of a giant, it would soon be exhausted with following your trail. Oh, dearest, do not run so far ahead of me, and rest a bit in love, that I may grasp you.

"O Lord, you who have withdrawn from me everything that I have from you, leave me by your mercy the same gift which you by nature have given to a dog; that is, that I may be faithful in my distress without rebellion. I truly desire this more than your heavenly kingdom."

God: "Dear dove, now hear me. My divine wisdom is so mighty over you that I allot all my gifts to you in such a manner as you can bear with your poor body. Your secret searching is bound to find me; your heart's misery can rightfully compel me; your sweet hunting makes me so tired that I desire to cool myself in your pure soul, into which I am bound. The sighing and trembling of your sore heart has driven my judgment away from you. So it is right for you and me. I cannot be without you. However we are dispersed, we cannot be separated. If I were to touch you ever so lightly, I would cause your body measureless pain. If I were to give myself to you at all times according to your desire, I would have to do without my sweet earthly dwelling in you; for a thousand bodies could not fulfill the desire of one living soul. That is why the higher a person is, the more he is a holy martyr."

The soul: "O Lord, you spare my impure prison far too much, in which I drink the water of this world and eat the ash-baked cake of my own weakness with great sorrow of heart. And I am wounded to death by the ray of your fiery love. And now, Lord, you let me lie unanointed in great torment."

God: "Dear heart, my queen, how long will you be so unruly? When I wound you most painfully, it is then I anoint you most inwardly. The fullness of my wealth is all yours, and you shall have might even over me. For you I pine; if the weights of the scale are yours, the gold is mine. All you have done, not done, and suffered for my sake, I will put that in the scale that will outweigh it, and will give myself to you for eternity, as much as you could ever want me."

The soul: "Lord, I wish to ask you about two things; teach me concerning them according to your mercy. When my eyes miserably mourn and my mouth is silent like a simpleton's and my tongue is bound in heart's sorrow and my senses ask me from hour to hour what ails me, then all that, Lord, is because of you. And my flesh falls away, my blood dries up, my bones freeze, my veins are clenched, and my heart melts for your love, and my soul roars with the voice of a hungry lion. How it is with me then, where you are then, my dearest, please tell me."

God: "You are like a young bride from whom the only one she loves, to whom she has inclined with all fidelity, has departed while she sleeps, and she cannot bear for him to leave her for an hour, and when she awakes, she has no more of him than that which she bears in her senses. Therefore her great lament begins. As long as the youth has not been given in marriage to his bride, she must often be without him. I come to you according to my pleasure, when I wish. You be gentle and still, and hide your sorrow where you can; then the power of love will increase in you. Now I will tell you where I am then. I am in myself in all places and all things, as I was from eternity without beginning, and I wait for you in the garden of love and pluck for you the flower of sweet union and make a bed for you there from the lovely grass of holy knowledge, and the bright sun of my eternal Godhead shines on you with the hidden wonder of my bliss, of which you have been allowed to taste a little in secret. And then I will bend down for you the highest tree of my holy Trinity, and break for you the green, white, red apples of my mild humanity, and then the shadow of my holy spirit will shelter you from all earthly sadness—then you will no longer be able to think of your heart's sorrow. When you embrace the tree, I will teach you the song of the virgins, the melody, the words, the sweet sound; those who are mingled with unchastity cannot understand these things alone of themselves, but one day they will all achieve the sweet transformation.

"Love, now begin and let me hear how you can sing."

The soul: "Alas, my well-beloved, I am hoarse in the throat of my chastity, but the sugar of your sweet mildness has made my throat to sound again, so that I can sing, therefore: Lord, your blood and mine is one and undivided; your garment and mine is one and immaculate; your mouth and mine is one bliss."

These are the words that the voice of love sang, but the sweet music of the heart cannot be given here, for no earthly hand can write it.

MECHTILD VON HACKBORN (1242–1299)

OF DIVERSE PAINS

When she had remained for more than seven days in this abandonment (sick and without "God's visit"), the most kind Lord, who is always close at hand to the heavyhearted, poured out upon her such overflowing comfort and sweetness that she often lay with closed eyes, as if dead, from matins to prime and from prime to nones, in the enjoyment of God. In this time the gentle Lord revealed to her the wonderful things of his mysteries and gladdened her so much with the sweetness of his presence that she, as if drunken, could no longer contain herself and imparted to guests and friends that inner grace that she had concealed for so many years. Therefore many gave her messages to God; and to each of them, insofar as God vouchsafed her the knowledge, she disclosed his heart's desire, for which they thanked God with great gladness.

When she complained that the pain in her head had deprived her of sleep, people said that her mind was wandering in her sickness, for they thought that she did nothing but sleep. But when her servant asked her what she did when she lay thus with closed eyes, she answered, "My soul delights in the enjoyment of God, swimming in the Godhead like a fish in water or a bird in the air; and there is no difference between the saints' enjoyment of God and my soul's union, except that they enjoy him in joy, and I in pain."

In these days of her illness, when the time of the fast arrived and she had resolved to be in spirit with the Lord in the wilderness, she asked him one night, when it seemed to her as if she were with the Lord in the wilderness, where he wanted to stay for the first night. Then the Lord showed her a wondrously beautiful but hollow tree, which was called the Tree of Humility, and said, "Here I will stay overnight." When he had said this, the Lord went into the hollow tree.

Then she said, "And where shall I stay?"

Then the Lord said, "Do you not know how to fly into my lap and rest there as the birds do?"

And immediately she saw herself in the form of a bird flying into the lap of the Lord, and she rested there very peacefully. And she said to the Lord: "O mildest Lord, lay your finger on my head that I may sleep."

And the Lord said, "Do you not know that the birds, when they want to receive sleep, lay their heads beneath their plumage?"

And she said, "Lord, what is my plumage?"

He answered, "Your desire is a red feather, because it is always burning. Your love is a green feather, because it is always green and growing. Your hope is a yellow feather, because you are constantly hastening toward me."

OF THE POWER OF LOVE

At another time, when in the working of grace she was thinking of the power of divine love, the Lord spoke to her: "See, I give myself into the power of your soul, so that I am your prisoner and you command me whatever you will; and I, like a prisoner who can do nothing save what his lord commands, am ready to do anything you wish."

She, receiving with wondrous gratitude the words of such favor, bethought herself what she might best desire of God's love. She found in her heart that she would like nothing better than health, for Easter was close at hand and she had not entered the choir since Advent, except at Christmas, because of her constant sickness. But communing with herself, and compelled by faithfulness to the Lord, she said to him, "O sweetest and most beloved of my soul, although I could now regain all the strength and health I ever had, I by no means wish it. Rather I wish this one thing from you: that I may never be at odds with your will, but that I may will with you whatever you will and work in me, be it advantageous or adverse."

Immediately it seemed to her that the Lord embraced her with his left arm and bent her head upon his breast and said to her, "Because you will all that I will, your soul will always be in my embrace, and all the pain of this head I will draw into myself and offer up with my suffering."

OF THE EMBRACE AND THE HEART OF THE LORD

Another time, when she complained to God in her sickness that she could not go into the choir or do other good works, it seemed to her that the Lord lowered himself into the bed beside her, embracing her with his left arm, so that the wound of his loving heart was bound up with her heart. Then he spoke to her: "When you are sick, I embrace you with my left arm, and when you have recovered, with my right. But know this: when you are embraced by my left arm, my heart is much more closely joined to you."

How God gives his senses to the soul that it may use them

She once begged the Lord to give her something that would always cause her to remember him. Thereupon she received from the Lord this answer: "See, I give you my eyes, that you may see all things with them, and my ears, that you may hear all things with them; my mouth I also give you, so that all you have to say, whether in speech, prayer, or song, you may say through it. I give you my heart, that through it you may think everything and may love me and all things for my sake." In these words God drew this soul entirely into him and united with it in such a way that it seemed to her that she saw with God's eyes, and heard with his ears, and spoke with his mouth, and felt that she had no other heart than the heart of God. This she was also given to feel on many later occasions.

GERTRUD VON HELFTA (1252–1302)

Of the loveliness of the indwelling of the Lord

When you did thus to me and summoned my soul, I went into the yard before Prime one morning between Easter and Assumption, and sat down by the pond and contemplated the loveliness of this place, which pleased me well because of the clarity of the water that flowed past, the greenness of the trees standing round, the freedom of the birds that flew about, especially the doves, but above all because of the sequestered quiet of the hidden seat. I began to consider in my soul what I would like to add to these things in order that the enjoyment of this place might seem perfect to me, and this I asked: that the familiar, loving, close-nestling, companionable friend were present to assuage my solitude. Then, O author of priceless blisses, you, my God, who as I hope guided the beginning of this meditation, you also drew the end toward yourself and instilled in me this thought: When out of the inflowing of

your grace I pour myself back into you like water with inexhaustible gratitude; when I grow in the exercise of the virtues and flour-
ish in the green of good works like the trees; when gazing from
above upon earthly things I strive toward the heavenly in free flight
like the dove, and, estranged with these bodily senses from the
commotion of outward things, devote myself to you with my whole
spirit—then my heart will give you a place that is more precious
than all loveliness.

When I knelt down to pray before going to sleep that evening,
having been absorbed all day in thoughts of these things, this
passage came into my mind: "He who loves me will keep my word;
and my Father will love him, and we shall come to him and make
our dwelling with him." Then my earthly heart in me felt that you
had come and were present.

OF THE DIVINE INFLOWING

When I thought that I was writing so incoherently, so that I could
not agree with my own conscience about it and had therefore put
off committing this to writing until the Exaltation of the Cross,*
and had decided on that same day, during mass, to turn myself to
other things, God led my spirit back with these words: "Know for
a certainty that you will never get out of the dungeon of the flesh
until you have also paid this penny you are now withholding." And
when I urged in my soul that I had kept all that God had bestowed
on me for the salvation of others, if not through writing, at least
through speech, the Lord cast up to me the word I had heard read
the same night at matins: "If the Lord had made known his teaching only to those present, there would be only speech, not writing.
Now, however, there is also writing for the salvation of the many."
And the Lord added: "Without contradiction I want a sure testimony to my Divine love in your writing for these latter times, when
I have determined to do good to many."

Burdened by this, I began to consider in myself how difficult,
even impossible, it would be for me to find such meaning or such
words with which that which is often said may be given over to the

---

*Annual festival taking place on the 14th of September in celebration of the
discovery of the Cross in Jerusalem by Queen Helena on 13 September 335 C.E.,
who on the following day revealed it by "elevating" it before the assembled public
(editor's note).

human mind without offense. The Lord, who gives help against such faintheartedness, seemed to pour an over-rich rain upon my soul, under whose violent downpour I, a mere little human being, so young and tender a plant, bent and sank down and could drink in nothing of use, except a few very difficult words whose meaning I could no means arrive at with my sensual understanding. Burdened still more by this, I considered what might come of such things. This burden you lifted from me by your kind love, O God, with the usual caress and revived my soul with these words: "Because the inundation of these floods does not profit you, I will only lean you against my Divine heart and pour the word into you softly, mildly and gradually, according to the measure of your comprehension."

This most true promise you have faithfully fulfilled, Lord my God. For four whole days, in the early morning, at the most suitable hour, you let flow into me always one part of the discourse, so clearly and gracefully that I could write what I had previously not thought, without any effort, like something long held in memory. You did it, however, with this moderation, that I, when I had set down one coherent part, could not by the most extreme effort of all my senses find out one word of what came to my hand the next day so flowingly and without any difficulty. So you instructed and restrained my turbulence, as Scripture teaches: No one should be so attached to activity that he cannot give himself to contemplation. You aroused my salvation and granted delay, so that I might rejoice in the sweet embraces of Rachel, without lacking Leah's honored fruitfulness. May your wise love grant that I may perform both to your satisfaction.

HEINRICH SEUSE (ca. 1295–1366)

At the beginning it occurred once on Saint Agnes's day that, when the convent had finished its midday meal, he went into the choir. He was alone there and stood in the lower pew of the right-hand choir. At the same time he had a strange oppression of heavy suffering that lay upon him. And as he stood disconsolate and no one was with him or around him, his soul was entranced, in the body or outside the body. There he saw and heard what no tongue can express. It was formless and without mode and yet had in it the joyful pleasure of all forms and modes. The heart was avid and yet satisfied, the mind happy and in a good state; all wishing was stayed and all desiring lost. He did nothing but stare into the splendid reflection in which he gained a forgetfulness of himself and of all things. He knew not whether it was day or night. It was a sweetness of eternal life that burst forth in a feeling of presence motionlessly at rest.

Afterward he said, "If this is not the kingdom of heaven, I do not know what the kingdom of heaven is; for all the suffering that could be put into words cannot rightfully earn this joy for him who is to possess it eternally." This overpowering entrancement must have lasted an hour or half an hour; whether the soul remained in the body or was separated from it, he did not know. When he came to himself again, he felt in every way like one who has come from another world. The body had such great pain from that brief instant that he did not believe any human could suffer so much pain in so short a time without dying. He came to himself with a sigh from the very depths, and the body sank down to the ground against his will, like one who collapses in a faint. He screamed within himself and sighed in the inner ground of himself and said, "Alas, God, where was I, where am I now?" and said, "Ah, my heart's treasure, this hour will never pass away from my heart."

He went about in the body, and no one saw or noticed anything about him outwardly, but soul and sense within him were full of heavenly wonder; the heavenly glimpses went to and fro in his innermost inwardness, and he felt as if he were floating in the air. The powers of his soul were full of sweet heavenly fragrance, as when one pours a good balsam out of a container, and yet the container keeps the good smell afterward. This heavenly fragrance remained with him for a long time afterward and gave him a heavenly longing for God.

One day at table the passage on Wisdom was read, and it stirred his heart to the depths. She spoke thus: "As the fair rose tree blossoms and the noble unmingled incense wafts its scent and the unmixed balsam its fragrance, so I am a blossoming, fragrant, unmixed truelove without rue and without bitterness in a lovesome sweetness deep as the abyss. But all other sweethearts have sweet words and bitter wages, their hearts are the dragnets of death, their hands are fetters of iron, their speech a sweetened poison, their sport a theft of honor.

He thought, "Ah, how true all this is!" and spoke more boldly in himself, "Truly, it must be so, she must surely be my true love, I will be her servant." And he thought, "Ah God, when shall I see my love, when shall I receive her speech? Ah, what is the sweet form of that which has hidden so many lovely things in itself? Is it God or human, woman or man, secret knowledge or magic power, or what may it be?"

And as far as he could see with his inner eyes in the parables Scripture presents, she appeared to him thus: She hovered high above him on a throne of clouds, she beamed like the morning star and shone like the playing sun; her crown was eternity, her garment was bliss, her word was sweetness, her embrace the fulfillment of all desire. She was far and near, high and low, present and yet hidden; she made herself accessible, yet no one could grasp her. She reached above the highest point of the highest heaven and touched the deepest part of the abyss. She spread out mightily from end to end and reconciled all things in sweetness.

Just when he was sure she was a beautiful maiden, at once he found a splendid youth. Sometimes she behaved like a wise instructor, sometimes she bore herself like a stately sweetheart. She bent down lovingly toward him and greeted him with much smiling and spoke kindly to him, *"Praebe, fili, cor tuum mihi!"* [Give me your heart, my son!] He bent down at her feet and thanked her heartily from the bottom of his humility. This was given to him then, and more could not be given to him at that time.

When during this period he would sometimes approach in his thoughts the loveliest one of all, he asked himself an inward question and asked his love-seeking heart thus: "Ah, my heart, see whence flow love and all that is lovely? Whence comes all tenderness, beauty, heart's desire, and gracefulness? Does it not all come from the overflowing source of the pure Godhead? Well then, heart and mind and mettle, let us plunge into the bottomless abyss of all beautiful things! Who will hold me back now? Oh, I embrace you today according to the desire of my burning heart!" And then the original outflow of all goodness impressed itself in his soul, and in this he found in spirit all that was beautiful, lovely and desirable; this was all in an ineffable manner.

By this he acquired the habit, that whenever he heard songs of praise being sung, or sweet music of strings playing, or songs of temporal loves being said or sung, his heart and mind were suddenly, with a detached inward gaze, led into his precious sweetheart, from whom all love flows. How often his heart's darling, with eyes weeping from love, with wide-open, abyss-deep heart, was embraced and pressed ardently to his loving heart, can never be told. It made him feel exactly as when a mother holds her suckling child in her arms and stands it on her lap: Just as the child leaps toward the caressing mother with its head and the movement of its little body and shows the joy of its heart with these smiling gestures, so his heart in his body was often moved, with a flowing of his inner being, toward the gladsome presence of eternal Wisdom.

He thought then, "O my God, if a queen were wed to me, my soul would enjoy it, but now you are my heart's empress and the bestower of all grace! In you I have riches enough, as much power as I could desire. Of all that the earth has, I would not have more!" And as he thought thus, his face became so joyful, his eyes so happy, his heart so jubilant, and all his inner senses sang the *Super salutem:* "Over all happiness, over all beauty, you the happiness and beauty of my heart; for with you happiness has come to me and I possess all that is good in you and with me."

When after matins, according to his custom, he had gone into his chapel and was sitting there for a rest in his chair—this sitting was short and lasted only until the watchman announced the dawning day—then his eyes were also opened and he fell quickly upon his knees and greeted the bright morning star as it rose, the tender queen of the heavenly kingdom, and felt that just as the little birds in summer greet the bright day and receive it joyfully, so he was greeting with joyful desire the light-bringer of the eternal day; and he did not simply speak the words then, but he spoke them with a sweet, quiet ringing in his soul.

Once when he was sitting and resting thus at that time, he heard a song begin within him with such feeling that his whole heart was moved, and the voice sang in pure, sweet, ringing tones, while the morning star rose, and it sang these words: *"Stella Maria maris hodie processit ad ortum."* [The star of the sea Maria has come forth today.] This song rang out in him with such supernatural beauty that his whole spirit was carried away and he sang happily along with the voice. When they had joyfully finished singing it together, he felt an ineffable embrace, and amid it he heard the words: "The more lovingly you embrace me and the more incorporeally you kiss me, the more lovingly and affectionately you are embraced in my eternal clarity." Then his eyes opened, tears streamed down his face, and he greeted the morning star according to his custom.

It was in the night of the Feast of All Angels that it seemed to him in a vision that he heard the song of angels and sweet heavenly music. This did him so much good that he forgot all his suffering. Then one of them said to him: "See, as glad as you are to hear the song of eternity from us, so glad are we to hear the song of eternal Wisdom from you." And then he spoke again: "This is from the song that the chosen saints will joyfully sing on the Judgment Day, when they see that they are confirmed in the everlasting joy of eternity."

Another time, on that same feast night, he had spent many hours in such contemplation of their joys, and toward dawn there came a youth who bore himself as if he were sent to him as a heavenly minstrel from God. With him came many splendid youths, with the same manner and bearing as the first, except that the first had more dignity than the others, as if he were an angel prince. This youth came blithesomely toward him and said that they had been sent down to him from God in order that they might bring him heavenly joy in his suffering; he bade him put his sufferings out of his mind and bear them company, for he must dance a heavenly dance with him. They took the servant by the hand for the dance, and the youth sang a joyful carol of the baby Jesus, that begins, *"in duci jubilo."*

When the servant heard the beloved name Jesus sounding so sweetly, his heart and his mind became so blithesome that all the suffering he had ever had vanished away. Now he saw with joy how they made the highest and freest leaps. The singer knew well how to make them move, and he sang and they sang after him and danced with hearts of rejoicing. The leader sang the refrain three times: *"Ergo merito."* This dancing was not of a kind with the dancing of this world; it was a heavenly wave that swelled outward and then again inward, into the wild abyss of the divine mystery. This and similar heavenly comforts were vouchsafed to him in these years in unspeakable measure, and most of all at those times when he was surrounded by unspeakable sufferings, and thus it was made easier for him to bear them.

CHRISTINA EBNER (1277–1355)

At a time when she was twenty-four years old she dreamed that she was pregnant with our Lord, and she was so full of grace that there was no limb of her body that did not feel particular grace from it. And she came to feel such tenderness for the babe, because she herself sheltered it, as it seemed to her, that once, when she had stepped upon a little rise in the ground, she feared that it might have hurt the child. And as this was in sweetness without any discomfort, so that no sorrow and no sadness touched her, she dreamed that she should bear him without any pain, and she received boundless joy from the sight of him. And when she had gone about for some time with this joy, she could conceal it no longer, and she took the child in her arms and carried it to those assembled in the refectory and said, "Rejoice with me; I can no longer conceal my joy from you; I have conceived Jesus and have now given birth to him." And she showed them the child. And as she was thus in great joy, she awoke.

He said, "I will look upon you with my merciful eyes. I will enrich you with my riches, I will exalt you with my exaltation." He said, "What more shall I do for you? I have done such great miracles for you that it is incredible to the heart. I have poured the treasure of my sweetness into you. You are one of the humans to whom I have given all that is most splendid from the beginning of the world. My kindness plays with all those whom I hold dear." Another day he said to her, "Those who in days to come shall read your writing should not be astounded by the wonderful things I have done for you. You have not deserved them of me. It was my pleasure to do them. I have it from my playing Godhead that I may do according to my pleasure. If I had a thousand worlds, then I would have enough to grant every person one kindness that I did not do for another."

One Friday he said to her, "I am your prisoner for love and come willingly to you. I will crown you with my mercy. I am the one who overcomes your senses." . . . On Saturday he said to her, "You will soon come to a place where all your misery will have an end. The divine stream that flows from me into the saints and laymen also flows into you and flows out of you again." . . . On Sunday he said, "I come to you as one who has died of love. I come to you with desire like a husband into his bridal bed. I come to you as one who gives great gifts." On Monday he said to her, "I am the overcomer of your senses." It was also said to her, "Behold him on whom the angels gaze." . . . On Saint Nicholas's Day he said to her, "I make you noble from my noble nature. I make you worthy from my nobility. I have bedewed you with the dew of divinity." On Friday he said, "My beloved, let me rest beside you, that I may forget my enemies. I will make your virtue rich." . . . On Saint Lucy's day he said, "I have kept all of a husband's fidelity toward you." . . . He said, "It comes of the playing of my divinity that I do good to you. It is bliss for me to do good to you." . . . He said, "My beloved, accept my speech lovingly, I speak now with no one so much as with you." On Saint John's Day he said, "I will do for you all that it is possible to do for a creature." He said, "I fill you with my divine sweetness, but I will gaze upon those who are present with my merciful eyes. Is it not a miracle from me that I show more grace to you than to those who live in the forests and in hollow trees and have a hard life, and yet I show you more grace?"

On Pentecost he said, "Heaven and earth must become aware of this day. I will bestow on you all that is good." By this he meant the particular grace that he gives to his friends. Then she asked him why he gave her such a great stream of sweetness. Then he said, "The world is continually in unrest. Therefore wherever I find a restful heart, I am glad to be there."

She asked him, "Dear Lord, have you ever made it known [the miracles that he worked with her] to any human being more than to me?" Then he said, "I have never made it so wholly known to a human being as to you. I have given you more sweetness than to a thousand other humans. I have drawn you out of yourself into a divine life. I have looked upon you as upon an image." She did not understand how he meant that. He answered her, "When I formed your soul in my divinity, it looked toward me and gazed at all the things that I wanted to do with you. Then my loving hand drew you toward me. I, the Lord of Mercy, have worked the miracle of miracles with you."

One day she partook of our Lord. Then he said, "My nobility has elevated you. My elevation has made you great. My affection plays with you. You are one of the humans on earth whom I now most greatly favor. I am a poor pilgrim. The heathens do not know me. The Jews do not want me. There is such confusion in the Christian lands that they do not perceive me. Where I find a willing heart, I play in it like the sun in itself."

On the holy eve of Easter . . . the favor of God increased in her heart with unspeakable richness, so that grace flowed from her soul into her body and into all her limbs, so that she was possessed and burdened by grace like a woman with child, and in this fullness of grace she remained for a long time.

He said, "I dwell in you as the fragrance in the rose. I dwell in you as the radiance in the lily. Noble fruit that I am, out of you I have blossomed."

MARGARETA EBNER (1291–1351)

Now when the hallelujah was rung at that time, I began to keep silence with the greatest joy, and especially in the night before Shrove Tuesday I was in great grace. And then it happened on Shrove Tuesday that I was alone in the choir after matins and knelt before the altar, and a great fear came upon me, and there in the fear I was surrounded by a grace beyond measure. I call the pure truth of Jesus Christ to witness for my words. I felt myself grasped by an inner divine power of God, so that my human heart was taken from me, and I speak in the truth—who is my Lord Jesus Christ —that I never again felt the like. An immeasurable sweetness was given to me then, so that I felt as if my soul was separated from my body. And the sweetest of all names, the name of Jesus Christ, was given to me then with such a great fervor of his love, that I could pray nothing but a continuous saying that was instilled in me by the divine power of God and that I could not resist and of which

I can write nothing, except that the name Jesus Christ was in it continually.

I have an image of the childhood of our Lord in a cradle. When I am so powerfully compelled by my Lord with such great sweetness and with pleasure and desire and also by his kind request, and it is also said to me by my Lord, "If you do not suckle me, I will withdraw from you, just when you love me the very most," then I take the image out of the cradle and lay it upon my naked heart with great pleasure and sweetness and feel then the most powerful grace with the presence of God, that I afterwards wonder how our Lady could ever have borne the constant presence of God. Then answer is given me with the actual words of the angel Gabriel: *"Spiritus sanctus supervenit in te."* But my desire and my pleasure is in the suckling, that I am cleansed by his pure humanity and inflamed from him with his ardent love, and his presence and his sweet grace pour through me, so that I am drawn thereby into the true enjoyment of his divine being with all loving souls who have lived in the truth.

On Saint Stephen's Day my Lord gave me a loving gift for my desire; for a lovely picture was sent to me from Vienna of Jesus in a cradle, with four golden angels waiting on him. And it was given to me by the child one night that I saw it playing by itself in the cradle with joy and lively gestures. Then I said to him, "Why won't you be a good child and let me sleep? I have bedded you well."

Then said the child, "I will not let you sleep. You must take me to you."

So I took him out of the cradle with desire and with joy and stood him on my lap. Then it was a living child. Then I said to him, "Kiss me, then I will overlook it that you vexed me." Then it threw its arms around my neck and embraced and kissed me.

When I thought of the visions afterward, I felt a new sweetness, and something began speaking in me in a new manner, with closed mouth and with inner words that no one understood or noticed except me. And these words made a sweet unformed voice in my mouth. These were the words: *"Ego vox clamantis in deserto,"* etc., and then, *"Fac me audire vocem tuam, vox tua dulcis,"* etc. And this happened to me often in that year. And then my mouth is closed by force, so that I cannot speak a word, though I should die. And this inner speech, of which I have written much, comes then with a joyous lightness out of my heart, and it begins just as when the master's skilled hand begins a lovely piece on a stringed instrument with a lovely prelude, and ends with a lovely postlude. And this time is supernaturally sweet to me: if there were no kingdom of heaven beyond it, I think that nevertheless I would have enough, and all creatures together could not move me from God by a hair's breadth.

ADELHEID LANGMANN (d. 1375)

Whatever was proper, pleasing, pious, and godly, the child kept, and was yet merry with people, without any boisterousness. When she went with her mother to the sermon, she locked in her heart's shrine whatever she heard there. When she then came home and was alone she contemplated what she had heard in the sermon, and especially the martyrdom of our Lord; this she contemplated very gladly, as much as she could. This was noticed by people who were near the child and took care of her. They often said to her mother, "That child belongs nowhere but in a convent."

This lasted until the child reached the age of thirteen. Then her relatives betrothed her to a young man. He became sick unto death. And when the wedding was to be celebrated and she sat upon the bridal chair, he lay in bed the whole day. So he grew sicker and sicker until the next year, when he died.

After that her relatives wanted to give her away again. Then our Lord said to a certain person, "Even if she were given to thirty men, they would all have to die. She must become mine." Then she asked good people to pray to God for her to let them know what his dearest will was. A good person was at devotions and prayed to God for her, asking whether it was his will that she should go into a convent. Then our Lord said, "Yes, it is my will. I want to have her where she is one with me."

Then the man said, "Lord, where is she one with you?"

Then our Lord said, "Where she is no one's."

Afterward, on the day of the apostles Philip and James, this person asked the holy apostles on her behalf, saying: "Dear saints, I ask you to inquire of our Lord concerning this maiden, whether it is his will that she should go into a convent."

Then the saints said, "Yes, it is his will that she should follow after us saints, and that she should abandon her own will, as we have done."

Then this person said to our Lord, "Lord, what will you give her for this?"

Then our Lord said: "I will give her the kingdom of heaven."

Now this young widow had the custom of taking seven severe disciplines each day, when her rightful bodily needs and her occupations permitted it. Now it occurred at Christmas that she received Our Lord on Christmas Day, and when she had our Lord in her mouth, he stuck so fast to her palate that she could not consume him. She drank, but it did not help her. Then she thought, "Dearest Lord, what have I done against your grace?"

Then our Lord in her mouth said to her, "You have done nothing against me. You must vow to me that you will go to the convent in Engeltal, then you will receive me."

Then she said, "Lord, that I will not do. I am too sickly, I cannot live poorly."

Then our Lord said, "Then you will not receive me." She thought that she would tell the priest, that he might help her. Then our Lord answered her thoughts and said, "Neither priest nor all who are in the church can help you to receive me unless you make me this vow." She thought she would vow it to him and then ask the priest to absolve her from her vow, since she would have made it against her will. Then our Lord answered against her thought and said, "That is not how I want it. I want you to vow it to me with the intention of performing it, though it should cost your life."

She thought, "Lord, then I vow it to you, though it should cost me life." Straightway she received him. She said, "Lord, today I have given you my will and my young body. Shall I then be blessed in the convent?"

He said, "Yes, for I will never leave you, and I myself will help you out of all the sufferings you will ever encounter, and will do well by you as by my best beloved and will never be parted from you." Then and there the Lord took from her all transient things, and she became glad that she should go to the convent.

THE SONG OF BARENESS

A CANTILENA FORMERLY ASCRIBED TO TAULER

I will sing of bareness a new song,
for true purity is without thought.
Thoughts may not be there,
so I have lost the Mine:
I am decreated.
He who is unminded has no cares.
My unevenness no longer causes me to err:
I am as gladly poor as rich.
I want nothing to do with images,
I must stand free of myself:
I am decreated.
He who is unminded has no cares.

Would you know how I escaped the images?
I perceived the right unity in myself.
That is right unity
when neither weal nor woe displaced me:
I am decreated.
He who is unminded has no cares.

Would you know how I escaped the mind?
When I perceived neither this nor that in myself,
save bare divinity unfounded.
Then I could not longer keep silent, I had to tell it:
I am decreated.
He who is unminded has no cares.

Since I am thus lost in the abyss
I no longer wish to speak, I am mute.
The Godhead clear has swallowed me into itself.
I am displaced.
Therefore the darkness delighted me greatly.

Since I have thus come through to the origin,
I may no longer age, but grow young.
So all my powers have disappeared
and have died.
He who is unminded has no cares.

> Then whosoever has disappeared
> and has found a darkness
> is so rich without sorrow.
> Thus the dear fire
> has consumed me,
> and I have died.
> He who is thus unminded has no cares.

FROM THE GERMAN SISTER-BOOKS (THIRTEENTH AND FOURTEENTH CENTURIES)

FROM THE ADELHAUSEN CONVENT IN FREIBURG, CHRONICLE OF ANNA VON MUNZINGEN

Else von Neustadt

There was a sister named Else von Neustadt who had been some seventy years in the convent, and a few years before her death she took to her bed and became so lame that she could not walk a step. Then she had to be in a separate chamber and was left so much alone there that she had little conversation with people, only enough to take care of her necessities. And with this sister God showed that he is a friend of all who are miserable and parted from all bodily comfort; this she confirmed to a sister who often came to her. The sister asked her whether she still thought of anything that was in this world. She said, "I have forgotten all things, but I can still remember God. I am also abandoned by all the world, but God has not abandoned me; he deals with me kindly and faithfully in every way. And especially since I have become so sick and helpless in my body, he has been especially gracious to me."

Then the sister asked her if it did not oppress her that her body was in such pain and bondage and that she was so completely isolated from people. She said, "I am as happy as a human being can be on earth. God has repaid me for my poor life and will do so more and more. How could one who sees God be vexed? He makes the time short and pleasant for me." Then the sister asked her whether she saw our Lord with outward or inward vision. She said, "I see him in both ways, outwardly and inwardly." The sister asked her again whether the outward or the inward vision was better and what the inward vision was like. She said, "The outward vision is nothing to the inward, for the inward vision is a full and very splendid thing." And again she said, "It is a divine vision, of which no one can say anything except the one who sees it, and even those who see it cannot speak of it rightly." Then the sister asked her if she could remember anyone. She said, "I cannot even remember myself very well. Where the mind and heart go, save only into him, I do not know. My soul then places itself in God and knows all things in him, and then I see the purity of my soul and that it is without any stain."

Then the sister asked her what he was like whom she saw with outward vision. She said, "He appears to me like a beautiful loving youth, and the chamber becomes crowded with angels and saints. He sits beside me and looks at me very kindly. But all the angels stand before him; he never comes alone, the angels always come with him. And he says to me, 'I will come again and again and soon I will take you to me and will never be parted from you in eternity.' And he embraces me with an inward embrace." Then the sister asked her what sort of garment he had on, and mentioned all kinds of colors. But she could not compare it to any color, but said, "Whatever he wills appears on him."

She had resigned her will so completely to his will that she desired neither to live nor to die, but just as he willed, and she would often say: "If it were sweet to God and pleased him, I would gladly endure this pain until the Judgment Day." And when she was in especial grace she was very merry and said very lovely words about God, and she said these words very often: "God is in me and I in him; he is mine and I am his; he belongs to me and I to him. My soul is beautiful and splendid and blithesome, for God has opened up his grace to me, and I am loved by him. This he has made known to me in his glory." Then the sister asked her what his speech was like when he spoke with her. She said, "His speech is so loving that no one can tell of it. He can speak so that it goes through the soul and through the bottom of the heart."

She also said very often: "God is in my heart and in my soul and seldom leaves me; only sometimes he flees from me, which he can do very well, then I chase after him with my spirit and am then so merry. And I say, 'Dear love, my sweetheart.'" Many such words, which were very friendly and loving, she spoke of God. The sister also asked her how she felt it when God was in her soul. She said, "I feel it by all the joy and bliss that he brings with him. He gladdens and widens my heart and opens my soul for me and unlocks it with his divine mercies." Then she asked her how one could arrive at such familiarity with God. She said, "When one loves him with complete fidelity and casts off all sin and everything becomes a praise of God—that is how it happened."

When she could not live much longer because of her age and sickness, the sister said to her, "Alas, what lives in you?" She said, "God lives in me and I in him." And when she was about to die the sister asked her how she felt. Then she showed her as well as she could that she was very ill in body and very blithe at heart. Then she asked her what she was glad of. She said, "I am glad of God, that he is mine and I his. He has said to me that he will take me to him, and all the fear and terror that I had of death and pain are entirely gone from my heart."

The sister also said to her, "How should we, your particular friends, conduct ourselves when you die?"

Then she said, "You shall laugh and be merry, for heaven is opened to me." Then she closed her eyes and lay as if she lay in sleep. And the sister called to her and asked if she were sleeping. She said, "I do not sleep, my rest is in God." Then she began to feel great pain, for death was approaching. Then the sister admonished her not to be dismayed by the travail, for God would soon make an end. She answered that it did not dismay her; however long God wished to draw out her travail, she would gladly suffer it. So she departed holy and blessed in the confidence that she would soon come to God.

Anna von Selden

It was her custom that whatever she desired of God, she would never stop asking him for it until he granted it to her. And once she came to such union with God in her prayer that God appeared to her so clearly that for five weeks afterward, whatever she saw, she thought it was God.

Berchte von Oberriet, the Elder

When she was about to die, she lay in prayer and told the praises of our Lord's martyrdom, as was her custom. And it seemed to her as if she were led to a field where people were about to martyr God, and there was a great call that she heard: "Will anyone let himself be hanged and martyred for God?" Then she called out, "Yes, I, gladly." And at that very moment death struck her, and her devotion remained until her soul left her body. Then she said the words: "Lord, I am hanging on your back, you'll have to shake me off, I'll never leave you." And in that devotion she departed.

Ita von Nellenburg

She said, "All that is in me is God, and between me and God there is nothing but the body."

Metze (Mechthild) Tüschel

She stood once before the altar and desired with her heart that she and God might become one thing. After much desire that she had, she said, "Lord, you created me for this; surely it is more fitting for you to dwell in my soul than in the pyx." Then a voice spoke to her: "When you become as empty and as rid of outward things as this pyx is empty of all things save me alone, then I will live in you, as essentially as in this pyx."

Berchte von Oberriet, the Younger

She had a very blessed life. And once she was in a great desire that God should do her particular grace, and in this desire she was so filled with overflowing grace that she could not speak of it, only that it seemed to her that her soul was wider than the whole world. And while the grace was so powerful in her, she desired of our Lord that he might let her see with bodily eye the miracle that was in her soul. Then it seemed to her as though she was like a full cask when the bottom is struck out of it, as though the entire grace were leaving her through her mouth. And this grace was the most rapturously beautiful child that a human eye ever saw. And for a long time she had very great joy with the child. But the grace and the joy that she had with the child were only a thousandth part as great as when the grace was in her. And she desired of our Lord that he should give her back the grace which she had had before and which was so very great when it was in her. Then our Lord withdrew from her both graces, so that she no longer saw the child, nor did the earlier grace return to her.

Reinlind von Villingen

She had a desire that she would have liked to know how her soul pleased God; and once when she was at her devotions she saw her soul as pure as crystal. And she saw that God was united with her soul, like a pure light.

FROM THE TÖSS CONVENT NEAR WINTERTHUR, ELSBET STAGEL'S SISTER-BOOK

Sofia von Klingnau

When she had lasted out the year with great bitterness, she told no one what consolation she had received from God, until she was close to death and had not much longer to live. Then a sister came to her with whom she had long been on terms of intimate affection and who had often observed that she was comforted by God. This sister begged her earnestly to tell her for the love of God how the comfort was which she had received from God. Thereupon she answered and said, "If I knew that it was God's will, I would tell you something. However, I do not know it; therefore I cannot tell you anything now. Come back soon; then I will tell you what is God's will." So the sister went away and waited until after the singing of the compline, when it was night, and then came to her again and asked her what had been the result of her consultation with God.

Then she said, "Lift me up and give me some water in my mouth so that I can speak; then I will tell you what you will be glad to hear." When this had been done, she began to speak and said, "In the second year after I had taken the vow of obedience, at the feast of the holy nativity, I stayed after midnight mass in the choir and went behind the altar and leaned against a prayer stand and tried to say my prayer as I was accustomed to doing. And while I was praying my former life came into my mind, how much time and how long I had spent in the world in frivolous pursuits. And I began especially to contemplate and consider the faithlessness I had thereby shown to God, that I had cared so negligently for the noble and dignified treasure of my noble soul, for which he had shed his holy blood on the cross and which he had commended to me so faithfully; and I had defiled and sullied it with so much sin and unvirtue, so that this soul which had once pleased him well must now be ill-pleasing and loathsome to his divine eyes. And from this thought I came into such great remorse that my heart became full of bitter and unaccustomed torment, and the torment increased so greatly in me that it seemed to me that I was feeling physical suffering and pain, as if my heart had a physical wound.

"In this pain I called upon my God with sighs of lamentation, saying, 'Woe, woe is me that I ever angered you, my God! If I could undo that, then I would choose that a pit might be here before my eyes reaching down to the abyss, and a post driven into it reaching up to heaven, and that I might be struggling up that post until the Judgment Day; I would gladly suffer that travail in exchange, my God, for never having angered you!' While I was in this will and in this desire for God, the torment and pain that was in my heart began to increase so mightily that I felt I could not bear it, my heart would break in two. Then I thought, 'Stand up and see what God wants to do with you.' And when I stood up, the pain was so great and the torment so overwhelming that all bodily strength and all sense failed me, and I fell down with no control over myself and fell into a swoon, so that I could neither see nor hear nor speak. And when I had lain thus as long as it was God's will, I came to myself again and stood up; but as soon as I stood up, I collapsed again, and again fell into a swoon, and this happened again a third time.

"And this time when I came to myself I began to be anxious, thinking that if I remained in that place for a while, the sisters might discover me and realize what had happened to me. And therefore I begged our Lord that he might give me sufficient strength that I might go to a secret place where no one would see or notice what I was going through. And so I stood up, and with great effort I came before the altar and stood up and said to the Lord, 'O Lord, my God, now I beg you for mercy: Now I recognize that I myself am wholly unworthy of all the mercies that you do for any of earth's creatures, and consider myself as more unworthy and more despicable before your eyes than a worm that crawls upon the earth, for the worm does not anger you, but I have angered you beyond measure; therefore I dare not ask, but commit myself wholly to your divine mercy.' And when I had said this, I bowed low and went to my bed in the dormitory; there, so it seemed to me, I would be most hidden. And when I had reached my bed, I was so very sick that I thought, 'You are ill again, you had better rest a while.' And therefore I made the sign of the cross before me and wanted to lie down to rest and said the verse *In manus tuas.*

"And when I had said it, I saw that a light, beautiful and blissful beyond measure, was coming from heaven, and it surrounded me and shone through me and illuminated me entirely, and my heart was transformed all of a sudden and filled with an unspeakable and strange joy, so that I utterly and completely forgot all the misery and torment that I had ever known until this time. And in the light and in the joy, I saw and sensed that my God was taken up from my heart and out through my mouth and high into the air, and there it was given me to see my soul clearly and particularly with spiritual vision, as I have never seen anything with physical eyes, and all its form and grace and beauty was shown to me fully. And what marvels I saw and recognized in it, all humans together could not put into words."

Then the sister adjured her by all fidelity and begged her in all earnestness to tell her what the soul was like. Then she answered and said, "The soul is so entirely spiritual a thing that one cannot really compare it to any physical thing. But because you desire it so much, I will give you a parable which may help you understand a little how its form and shape was. It was a round, beautiful, and illuminating light, like the sun, and was of a gold-colored red, and this light was so immeasurably beautiful and blissful that I could not compare it with anything else. For if all the stars in the sky were as big and beautiful as the sun, and if they were all shining together, all their splendor could not compare with the beauty my soul had. And it seemed to me that a splendor went out from me that illuminated the whole world, and a blissful day dawned over the whole earth. And in this light which was my soul, I saw God blissfully shining, as a beautiful light shines out of a beautiful radiant lamp, and I saw that he nestled up to my soul so lovingly and so kindly that he was wholly united with it and it with him. And in this union of love my soul acquired from God the certainty that all my sins had been wholly forgiven me, and that it was as pure and clear and wholly stainless as it was when I came out of the baptismal font. And from this my soul became so blithesome and joyful that it felt as if it possessed all bliss and all joy, and if it had the power of wishing it could not and would not wish for anything more. . . .

"And now, when I was in the best and highest joy, my soul began to sink down again, as God willed, until it hovered over the body, which was lying beside the bed like a corpse, and it was granted a delay, so that it did not have to reenter the body immediately, but had to hover for a considerable time over the body, until it had well seen how ugly and ill-formed the body was. And when the soul had gotten a good look at the body, and had seen how deathlike and wretched it was, and how its head and hands and all its limbs lay there like those of a dead person, it pleased her very ill, and seemed to her most loathsome and horrible. And very soon the soul turned its gaze from the body and gazed on itself. And when it saw itself again and found itself so beautiful and noble and dignified, in contrast to the body, it hovered over it, playing with such joy and delight that all hearts together could not imagine it. And just as it was feeling happiest and enjoying itself and God, with whom it saw itself united, it went back into the body, without knowing how. And when it had come back into the body, it was not deprived of this glad contemplation, but even while dwelling in the body it saw itself and God in it, as pure and essential as when it had been entranced out of the body.

"And this grace lasted in me for eight days, and when I came to myself again and became aware that a living spirit was in me, I stood up and was the most joyful person, so it seemed to me, on the whole earth. For all the joy that all humans ever gained or may gain until the Judgment Day seemed as small to me in comparison to my joy as the tiniest claw of a gnat in comparison to the whole world. And from the abundance of the measureless joy my body had grown so light and agile and so without any infirmity that for those eight days I never felt whether I had a body, so that I was not aware of any physical illness, small or great, and I had no hunger nor thirst nor desire for sleep, and yet I went to table and to bed and to the choir and did as the others did, so that my grace would be hidden and no one would notice it. And when I had passed these eight days in such bliss, the grace was withdrawn from me, so that I no longer had the contemplation of my soul and of God in my soul, and then for the first time I felt that I had a body."

Jützi (Lucia) Schultheiss

Then God decreed a great temptation for her, that she thought and it became her opinion that she should never see God. And thereby she came to such great contempt of herself that she did not dare to look up to heaven and she thought herself unworthy that the earth should bear her. And this lasted with her day and night, so that she had no respite, except that for her bodily needs she ate and slept a little. And in this great distress and travail she never abandoned her devotions nor the earnestness she had toward God, and increased still more in divine love, so that she wholly acquired the will never to cast off her exercises or her earnestness toward God, even if she should live until the Judgment Day, and even if she had no confidence that it was acceptable to God from her.

But through God's mildness all that she encountered benefited her, and whatever she saw or heard increased her love of God, and she praised him in her heart. When she saw any person behave as if they were happy, she thought, "God bless you, it is right that you are happy, for God has created and destined you to enjoy eternal bliss and the countenance of God, of which I, poor human being that I am, am unworthy." This torment she suffered from the day one ceases to sing hallelujah until Holy Thursday before matins. Then she felt very ill, for she had caught a new fever in addition to the sickness she had had before; and she was so sick that on that day she had not spoken the prayer as she was used to do. For it was her custom to say her prayers in the choir, often even when she was so sick that she could scarcely be brought into the choir; for it was her custom not to perform it elsewhere. And on this day she had omitted it because her sickness was overgreat.

And in the night, before matins, she sat up in bed and tried to say the prayer. Then she felt so ill she could not continue. And yet, not wanting to omit it, she began again. And then she heard a voice, which said to her very lovingly, "You are to rest and let me instruct you as to what you shall ask for." And then she took fright and feared that it was some deception. Then the voice spoke again the same words, and she was silent and listened. And then the voice spoke again: "You shall pray for your forgotten sins and for your untold sins and for your unrecognized sins and for the sins you cannot put into words. And then you shall pray that you may become one thing with him, as he was one thing with the Father before he became human. And you shall pray that there may never more be anything separating you and the Father. And you shall pray that as he became this day a coming and an eternal food for all Christendom, so may he become for you a coming and an eternal food. And you shall pray that he himself may come to your end and may accomplish all this and confirm it eternally."

From this she received great and measureless joy and gained strength of heart and body. Yet she seemed to herself unworthy of the grace and the comfort, so that she could not be altogether sure whether it was from God. And as matins approached, she remained at rest and was concerned about this, and she heard a voice above her head singing such boundlessly sweet German words that neither tune nor words could be compared to any physical things. And then she sat up and wanted to hear whether she could understand any of the words. And then the voice began to go away from her, so that she could not understand a single word. And whichever way she turned after the voice, it seemed to her to be coming from somewhere else, and she thought, "Lord God, I cannot think of anything this might be except your eternal goodness, that you want to assure me that I should have no doubt." And then she no longer heard the voice. And then the temptation was taken from her completely.

And afterward new miracles and new knowledge of God opened in her every day, so that she recognized clearly and distinctly all the miracles that God had ever worked in heaven and on earth. Moreover she was so wise in these hours that she recognized and understood all wisdom, in Scripture and in outward works; she understood it better than all the masters who had ever taught concerning it and concerning each particular thing. She also recognized clearly how the eternal Word had become flesh in the body of the Virgin. . . . And she saw directly how we have become his limbs and are joined and fastened to him as the limbs to the tree. . . . She also recognized. . . . how we are all equal to one another and altogether one thing, and how one human being owes all good to another as to himself. And the recognition that she had of all things that God has ever done and will yet do was as evident in each particular as it is to the angels in the kingdom of heaven, and she saw it as clearly as she was to see it after this life in eternity. And when this recognition of each thing approached, it passed by so that her heart never remained standing in it and she gained no comfort from it, as if it had never happened. She also recognized particularly how God is in all things and in all creatures. . . . She also saw how God is in every little blade of grass and in every blossom and leaf, and how he is everywhere around us and in us. . . .

Once she sat in her bed in great sickness and entered into great love and grace and came so close to God and desired such over-abundantly great things from God, that she heard a voice say, "How do you know that God has chosen you for this?" When she heard the voice she was so terrified that she began to despise herself so greatly that she was entirely annihilated. And she recognized that she was more despicable than a worm and that she had nothing that came from herself except sin. And in this great contempt of herself she yet recognized what God was, and found no place in herself nor in hell nor in heaven of which she deemed herself worthy except at the very bottom of hell. . . . In this state she remained until morning, at mass. Then she heard once more an inner voice that spoke and made known to her more loudly the Word that had been given to her in the prayer, that he and the Father were one thing before he created man or became man; that this is nothing other than that he is one will and one love, and therefore she too should become with him one will and one love. And then she came into a state that remained constant and united her will with his. . . . She also beheld clearly what it is to see God face to face. Of this she could not speak. She also saw clearly and recognized how the Son is eternally born from the Father, and that all the joy and bliss there is rests in the eternal birth. How she penetrated deeper into the eternal nature of God, of this she could not speak, nor did she know it, for she had lost herself so completely that she did not know if she was human. But afterward she came to herself again and was a human being like any other and had to believe and do all things like any other human. . . .

In the seven years that God worked this miracle with her she did not come into a common room for five years, and she never remained for long with people when she could avoid it. And once it was very cold, so that the sister who was caring for her begged her earnestly to let herself be helped into the common room, while the sisters were at vespers. And then she said to her attendant, "Now you go to vespers and leave me here, so that God may have some praise from it," for it was a holy day. And when she remained thus alone she saw that our Lord came in, and he was the same age as when he walked upon earth and preached. And with him walked Saint John and Saint James the elder, and she recognized them together and each face in particular. And they led him as they would a lord, being careful as to who might approach him, and had put their arms around him, one arm before, the other behind. And as they entered thus, they let him out of their arms, and he stopped in front of them and said, "Now behold how my life was on earth!"

Then she saw clearly how full of suffering he was: his eyes were sunken, and his cheeks were pitiful to see from the immense sorrow that he suffered. And then he sat down with his back to her. And as he sat down she recognized that he was very weary from heavy labor, for his back and all his limbs cracked and he groaned within himself. And when he had sat down, Saint John and Saint James sat down beside him. And afterward she saw that the sisters were going in and out, yet none said, "God greet you!" or "What do you wish?" And this looked so despised and wretched that no heart could bear to see it. And as the sisters were going in and out thus, the disciples stood up; but our Lord stood still. She also saw that the robes of our Lord and Saint James were alike, and were red inside; that of Saint John, however, was not red inside, but outside it was like their robes. The disciples seemed to be in the best of health. And as she was in this vision, a sister came and

spoke with her and brought her to herself again, and then she saw
nothing more.

Ita von Sulz

Once she had been appointed keeper of the wine cellar, and this
grieved her sorely, for she feared that her devotions would be
disrupted. And she went into the choir and complained of it to the
Lord. He comforted her very lovingly and said, "I am found in all
places and in all things." And by this she was quite comforted and
received the office gladly, and our Lord was familiar with her and
did her as much kindness as ever.

Mezzi Sidwibrin (Mechthild Seidenweber)

How sweet her life was cannot be put into words. Only this much,
that her mouth overflowed with sweet words, her eyes continually
poured forth the sweet tears of love, and in word and deed she
conducted herself as if there were no one else except her and God.
Once she said with great love, "Lord, if you were Mezzi Sidwibrin
and I were God, I would let you be God and I would be Mezzi
Sidwibrin."

Anna von Klingnau

She had such zeal for ordinary work that she often did her spinning
in bed, and before her on the distaff she had these words:

> The sickly you are, the dearer you are to me.
> The more despised you are, the nearer you are to me.
> The poorer you are, the more you are like me.

She often spoke these words with desire and she said that God
spoke this to a certain person. But we think that she was the
person.

Adelheid von Lindau

We also had a very blessed lay sister called Sister Adelheid von
Lindau, who was about a hundred years old when she died, and
was altogether blind, and lay in bed for at least three years before
her death in such patience that her attendant said she had never
seen her impatient. And she prayed most zealously, so that the

attendant always found her praying night and day, and was so merry that she often sang little songs of our Lord in a blithesome manner. Sometimes she also spoke so lovingly with God as if he were sitting in her presence. Sometimes she said:

Ah, dear Lord, you are my father and my mother
And my sister and my brother.
O Lord, you are my desire alway,
And with your mother all day I play.

The Fourteenth Century in the North

BIRGITTA VON SCHWEDEN (ca. 1302–1373)

There were seen by the bride two devils standing at God's bar of judgment, similar to one another in all their limbs. Their mouths were wide open like those of wolves, their eyes blazing like a glass that is illumined from within, their ears hanging like dogs' ears, their bellies swollen and protruding much too far in front, their hands like a griffin's, their legs without joints, their feet as if maimed and hacked off in the middle. One of the devils said to the judge: "Judge, award me this knight's soul, which is similar to me, that I may unite with it as with a spouse." The judge answered: "Say, what justice and what proofs have you against this soul?" The devil answered: "First I will ask you, since you are just, whether it is not usual to say, when one beast is found to resemble another, that this beast is of lion kind or wolf kind or the like. Now I ask you, of what kind is this soul, or whom does it resemble, the angels or the devils?" The judge said: "It does not resemble the angels; it resembles you and the likes of you, as is plain enough to see." Then the devil said mockingly: "When this soul was created from the glow of the anointing, which is your love, it resembled you. But now it has despised your sweetness and has become mine by a threefold right. First, because it is the same as me in form and function. Second, because we have one and the same taste. Third, because we have one and the same will." The judge answered: "Although I know everything, yet say for the sake of my bride, who is present, how this soul resembles you in form and function." And the devil said: "As we have limbs of the same shape, so we have deeds of the same shape. For we have open eyes, but we see nothing. For I do not want to see anything that pertains to you and your love; and similarly this soul, when it could, did not want to see what pertains to you and the soul's salvation, but heeded only pleasurable and worldly things. Moreover we have ears, but we do not hear anything of use to us; similarly this soul did not want to hear anything pertaining to your honor, and similarly everything of yours is bitter to me; therefore the voice of your sweetness and excellence will never come into our ears to our comfort and profit. We have open mouths; for as this soul had its mouth open for all the dainties of the world, but closed for you and for what might honor you, similarly I always have my mouth open to what may offend and grieve you, and never will I restrain it from doing ill to you, if it were possible to destroy you or to transform you out of your glory. "This soul's hands are like the hands of a griffin; whatever it could grasp of earthly things it held fast in its grip until death, and would have gripped it longer, had you permitted it to live longer. So I too grip all who get into the hands of my power, so mightily that I would never let them go if they were not abducted from me against my will by your justice. Its belly is swollen because its greed stretched beyond measure, for it filled itself and was never satisfied, and so great was its greed that if it could have had the whole world for itself alone, it would have managed to swallow it and would have liked to rule heaven into the bargain. And I, too, have a greed just like it. For if I could win all souls in heaven and on earth and in purgatory, I would gladly snatch them. And if a single soul remained, because of my greed I would not leave it free from torment. Its breast is altogether cold, just like mine; for it had no love for you at all, and your admonitions were not to its taste; thus I too am not moved by any love toward you, rather by hate, and gladly would I perish in the bitterest death, in tortures eternally renewed, in order that you might be killed, if it were possible to kill you. The legs of both of us are' jointless, because our will is one. For from the beginning of creation my will was moved against you, and I never willed as you did. Similarly its will, too, was always against your commandments. Our feet are as if maimed, for just as one strides with the feet toward what may profit the body, so one strides with fervor and good works toward God. And just as this soul never wanted to stride toward you with fervor or with good works, neither did I. "Thus in the form and function of the limbs we are alike in every respect. We also have the same taste, for although we know that you are the highest good, we do not taste how sweet and good you are. Therefore since we are alike in all things, give your judgment for our union. . . . Is it not written in your law that where there is one will and one consent to marriage, a lawful union can occur? So it is between us, for our two wills are one. Why then should we be deprived of union?" The judge said: "Let the soul make known its will and what it thinks of the union with you." The soul answered the judge: "I would rather be in the torment of hell than enter into the joy of heaven, so that you, God, may have no comfort from me, for so hateful are you to me that I little mind my own torment, if only you are not comforted." Then spoke the devil to the judge: "Such a will have I also. For I would rather be tortured eternally than enter into glory, that you might have comfort of it." Then said the judge to the soul: "Your will is your judge, and you shall receive judgment according to your will."

In the night of the Lord's birth the bride of Christ experienced such a wonderful and great soaring of the heart that she was beside herself with joy. And in the same moment she felt in her heart a palpable and astonishing movement, as though in her heart a living child were rolling to and fro. When this movement continued, she indicated it to her spiritual father and a few spiritual friends, fearing that it might be some deception. They tested it by sight and touch and, wondering, acknowledged the truth.

Later that same day the mother of God appeared to her at high mass and spoke to the bride: "Daughter, you are astonished at the movement that you feel in your heart. Know that it is no deception, but a representation of the parable of my sweetness and the mercy that was shown to me. For as you do not know in what way the soaring of the heart and the movement came to you unexpectedly, similarly the coming of my Son into me was wonderful and swift. For when I had spoken my consent to the angel who announced the conception of the Son of God to me, I immediately felt in me something astonishing and alive. And when it was born from me, it came with unspeakable rejoicing and uncommon haste out of my closed virgin womb. Therefore, daughter, fear no deception, but rejoice, for this movement that you feel is the sign that my Son has come into your heart. And as my Son has given you the name of bride, I from now on will call you daughter-in-law. For as the father and the mother, as they grow older, lay the burden upon the daughter-in-law and instruct her in what is to be done in the house, so God and I, having grown old in the hearts of men and been chilled by their lovelessness, will proclaim our will to our friends and the world through you. But this movement of your heart will remain with you and will increase according to the capability of your heart."

JULIAN OF NORWICH

REVELATIONS DATED 1373

Our good Lord spoke to me, most blessedly: "Oh, how I love you!" as if he had said, "My dearest, wait and behold your God, who is your maker and your endless joy. Behold your own brother, your Savior, wait and behold what delight and bliss I have in your salvation. And for my love rejoice with me." This blessed word "Oh, how I love you!" was said as if he said, "Wait and behold that I loved you so much before I died for you that I wanted to die for you. And now I have died for you and suffered willingly all that I could. And now all my bitter pain and my hard wandering has become joy and bliss everlasting, for me and for you. How then could you ask me for anything pleasing to me, without my granting it to you gladly? For my pleasure is your holiness and your endless joy and bliss with me."

Because of the great, infinite love which God has for all humankind, he makes no distinction in love between the blessed soul of Christ and the lowliest of the souls that are to be saved. . . . We should highly rejoice that God dwells in our soul, and still more highly should we rejoice that our soul dwells in God. Our soul is made to be God's dwelling place, and the dwelling place of our soul is God who was never made. It is a high knowledge to see inwardly and to know that God, who is our creator, dwells in our soul. And it is a higher and more inner knowledge to see and to know that our soul, which is created, dwells essentially in God. From this essential dwelling in God we are what we are. And I saw no difference between God and our essence, but it was all God.

And this I saw with full certainty, that it is easier for us to acquire knowledge of God than to acquire knowledge of our own soul. For our soul is so deeply founded in God and so infinitely gathered in that we cannot acquire knowledge of it until we have knowledge of God, its creator, to whom it belongs. Yet I saw that it is needful for us to desire to know our own soul in wisdom and truth; and therefore we are instructed to seek it where it is, namely in God. And so we shall come to know them both in one through the gracious guidance of the Holy Spirit. Whether we are moved to know God or our soul, both are good and true. God is much closer to us than our own soul, for he is the ground in which our soul stands. . . . For our soul sits in God in true rest, and our soul stands in God in sure strength, and our soul is rooted in God in endless love. Therefore if we wish to acquire knowledge of our soul and enter into fellowship and covenant with it, we must seek it in God our Lord, in whom it is enclosed.

Our Lord opened my spiritual eye and showed me my soul in the middle of my heart, and I saw the soul as wide as if it were an infinite world, and as if it were a blessed kingdom.

Mysticism in the Netherlands

GERLACH PETERS (1378–1411)

Thanks be to you, you my light, you eternal light, you never-diminished light, you highest and immutable good, before whose countenance I stand, a poor and paltry slave.

Thanks be to you! Now I see; I see the light that shines in the darkness.

And what do you see in this light?

I see how mightily you love me; and that when I remain in you, it is as impossible that you should not be attached to me at all times, in all places and on all occasions, as it is impossible that I should ever be detached from you.

And you yourself give yourself to me wholly, so that you are wholly and undividedly mine, as long as I am wholly and undividedly yours. And if I am so wholly yours, then you have loved me from all eternity just as you have loved yourself from all eternity; for this is nothing else than that you enjoy yourself in me, and that I, by your grace, enjoy you in me and me in you.

And if I love myself so, then I love nothing other than you, for you are in me and I am in you as one single thing that has come into being through union and can never be divided to all eternity. And since each loves the good and the strength in the other, so this is nothing other than that you love yourself.

But if I remain wholly and completely in you, as you cannot perish, so I cannot perish.

One poor in spirit, strengthened by the Lord, spoke from the upper part of his spirit as follows:

See, I am rich and possess abundance; for I already have all I desire of this world; and even this that I have, I have as though I did not have it; for I do not possess it with love and could do without it, without losing anything of myself.

The highest, bare, imageless and immutable truth itself lives in the uppermost part of my spirit and shows me its inexpressible treasures, which cannot be compared to anything; the one simple Word in which everything is included and beyond which I seek nothing else.

There my nothingness and the nonbeing of myself as myself are shown to me; and all frailties that could incline the temper in any direction and also the true nature of all things are shown to me.

Moreover I do not contemplate from below the lower occurrences and accidents according to mutable sensuality; but from above I contemplate all things, and for me Truth calls down, with terrible voice, upon all the alienness that is not one with it: Approach not, for the place where she stands is holy.

And thus she often shows me her countenance, in the choir, on my bed, at table, in my cell, in the din that is without, at work and at various occupations; and she teaches me to simplify inwardly all things that are without, and to transform them into an inward and steadfast contemplation.

However, this countenance is so strong that it powerfully overwhelms heart and body, so that not only the foundations but also the heart-thresholds of the temple of God are moved to answer, to yield, to follow faithfully wherever the way leads, to follow with all their might the light that has been shown, and incessantly to sacrifice all that is and can be, along with all that has been created in time and eternity.

And at such times it would be a great consolation and relief to my heart if I could bow, prostrate myself, humiliate myself, and cast myself down, even with my body, beneath all that is created.

And the countenance almost annihilates me as myself, frail thing that I am: it shows me that everything that does not unite itself in the countenance is nothing.

And after I have been thus decreated, it takes my willing gaze, presses it into its own gaze, unites with it directly, so that my gazing and its gazing become a single clear gazing, which is not turned back from any side; and all that is and can be, I see in my manner, in it, and with it, as the countenance itself sees it.

Therefore I am unconcerned about myself and tranquil in all that may befall me. And whatever has permission to befall me from the immutable truth and eternal determination of my Lord—to whom I have surrendered my life and my death and all I am and can be, in time and eternity, not presumptuously feeling anything in advance, nor choosing anything for my ease—whatever it may be, I too give it permission to befall me.

The Italian Women

ANGELA DI FOLIGNO (1248–1309)

Once during Lent it seemed to me that I was very dry and without devotion. And I prayed God that, since I was empty of all good, he might give me of himself. And then the eyes of the soul were opened, and I saw love coming toward me. And I saw the beginning, but I did not see its end, only its continuation. And of its colors I can tell no comparison. And when love came to me I saw all this with the eyes of the soul, more unveiled than one can see with the eyes of the body. And love approached me in the form of a crescent. But this is not to be understood as meaning that the form was measurable in size; rather it was like a crescent because it first came close to me, then drew back, and did not impart itself in the same measure as it made itself known. And forthwith I was filled with love and an inexpressible contentment which, though it contented me, yet created the greatest hunger in me, so unspeakably great that all my limbs were slackened and the soul languished and desired to join the rest. And I did not want to see or hear or be aware of any creature. And I did not speak. But my soul spoke inwardly and cried out to love not to let her languish in such great love, for I regarded life as a death.

And when through the approach itself I thought that I myself was wholly the love that I felt, it said, "There are many who think they stand in love but stand in hatred; and on the other hand there are many who think they stand in hatred, but are in love." But my soul sought to see this in great certainty, and God allowed me manifestly to feel it, so that I was entirely satisfied. But I am so filled with that love that I do not believe I could ever do without it again. And a creature who said otherwise I could not believe; and if an angel said otherwise to me, I would not believe it, but would answer, "You are the one that fell from heaven."

And I saw in myself two sides, as if a road were made within me.

And on the one side I saw love and all that is good, and all that is of God and not of me; and on the other side I saw myself arid, and I saw that nothing good originated in me. And by this I saw that it was not I who loved, although I saw myself in love; but that which loved came from God alone, and around that which loved, love gathered itself and imparted a greater and more fiery love than before, and I had a desire to hasten toward that love. And between this love, which is so great that at that time I could not know that there could be a greater love, until that other deathlike love came over me—between pure love, then, and the other, deathlike love, which is the greatest of all—there is something in the middle, of which I can tell nothing: for it is of such great depth, and such great rapture, and such great joyousness, that it cannot be put into words.

And at that time I did not want to hear anything more about suffering, nor even that God should be mentioned in my presence; for when he is mentioned in my presence, I feel him with such delight that I am tormented with faintness from love, and everything that is less than he becomes an obstacle for me. And what is said of the Gospels or of the life of Christ or any talk of God seems to me as nothing, for I see incomparably greater things in God. And when that love has left me, then I remain entirely contented, angelic, so that I love toads and worms and even the devils. And when I am in that state, if a wild beast devoured me I would not care, and it would seem to me that I suffered no pain. And then even the remembrance and thought of Christ's suffering is not painful. Nor are there any tears in that state.

One time my soul was exalted, and I beheld God in such great clarity as I had never before beheld him and in so complete a manner as never before. And I did not see love in him, and I lost the love that I had borne earlier, and I became nonlove. And afterward I beheld him in a darkness; in darkness, because he is a greater good than can be thought or understood, and nothing that can be thought or understood can approach the good that he is. And at that time the soul acquired a faith of primal certainty, a confident, solidly founded hope, a constant surety given by God, so that it lost all fear. And in that good which is seen in darkness I gathered myself completely and became so sure of God that I could never doubt my possessing God in great certainty. And in that exceedingly effective good which is beheld in darkness, all my hope is gathered and sure. I often see God in this manner and in this goodness that cannot be told outwardly nor even grasped with the heart. In that altogether certain and closed-off good which I mean when I speak of the darkness that is so great, I have all my hope; and in gazing I have wholly whatever I wish to have; and whatever I wish to know I know wholly; and I see therein all that is good. And in gazing the soul is not able to think that this good is from her, nor that she must go away from it, nor that she would ever have to part from it, but she delights unspeakably in that whole good. And the soul sees nothing at all that she could tell with the mouth or comprehend with the heart; and she sees nothing, and yet sees all. And because that good is in darkness, it is all the more certain and all the more superior to all things, the more it is seen in darkness; and it is very hidden. And later I see in the darkness that it is superior to every good, and that all and everything else is dark beside it and everything that can be thought is less than this good.

And even this, when the soul sees the divine might, and when she sees the divine wisdom, and even this, when she sees the divine will, all of which I have seen in a wonderful and inexpressible manner, all this is less than that wholly certain good. For that good which I behold is the whole, but all these others are a part. And when these others are beheld, although they are inexpressible, they yet bring a great joy that pours into the body. But when God is seen in this way in darkness, it brings no laughter into the mouth, no fire and no devotion into the heart, and no burning love. For the body does not tremble and is not moved, nor yet changed, as is wont to occur in contemplation of the other aspects. For the body sees nothing, but the soul gazes, while the body rests and sleeps, and the tongue is cut off, since it then can say nothing.

And all the many and unspeakable acts of friendship that God has shown me, and all the sweet words he has given me, and all other gifts and deeds are so much inferior to that good that I see in the great darkness, that I do not set my hope on these things.

Rather, if it were possible that they were all not true, it would not diminish my hope in the least. . . .

And everything that I say of it seems to me as if I said nothing. Indeed, whatever I say, I feel as if I were saying something wrong, and my talk seems to me like a blasphemy. So greatly does that good transcend all my words.

And when I see that good, as long as I am in it, I do not remember the humanity of Christ, nor the God-man, nor any other thing that has form. And yet at the same time I see everything, and I see nothing.

But if I am separated from that good, then I see the God-man, and he draws the soul to him with such great mildness that he sometimes says, "You are I, and I am you." And I behold those eyes and that countenance so gracious that my soul is embraced and drawn to him with infinite fervor. And what breaks forth from those eyes and from that face is that good that I have said I see in darkness. And it streams forth and comes from within, and it is this that gladdens me so that it cannot be told.

And standing in the God-man, my soul lives; but I stand far more in him than in that darkness. Yet that good of the darkness draws the soul far more than that of the God-man, incomparably more. But in the God-man I stand almost constantly, so constantly that the certainty was once given to me from God that there is nothing intermediate between me and him, and since then there has not been a day or a night when I have not constantly had this joy of his humanity. And then I have the desire to sing and to praise God, and I say, "I praise thee, beloved God. Upon thy cross I have made my bed. And for pillow and featherbed I have found poverty, and for a bed of rest, pain and scorn. For upon this bed he was born, thereon he rested and thereon he died. And God the Father so loved this loving companionship with poverty, pain, and scorn that he gave it to his Son, and his Son wanted always to lie upon this bed, and loved it always, and was at one with the Father. And upon this bed I have rested and I rest; it is my bed, and thereupon I hope to die, and thereby I believe that I will be saved. And the joy that I await from those hands and feet cannot be named. For when I see him, I would like never to depart thence, but to come closer and closer; and so my life is a dying. And if I think of him, I cannot speak, for my tongue is cut off. And if I go away from him, the world and all that I find drive me to desire that bed still more. And so my longing is a deadly torment to me because of the melancholy of expectation.

Afterward I was elevated in the spirit and found myself altogether within God in another manner that I had never experienced. And it seemed to me that I was in the midst of the Trinity, in a higher and greater way than I had hitherto known; for I received greater goods than usual and was constantly in these goods and was full of the greatest and unspeakable joys and raptures that are far beyond all that I have ever experienced. Such nameless divine miracles occurred in the soul that no saint, no angel, can tell or explain them. And I understand that no angel nor any other creature is capable of grasping those divine workings and that bottomless abyss. And this which I say appears to me as evil talk and blasphemy. And I am drawn out of everything that I had before and in which I was wont to delight; that is, from the life and humanity of Christ, and from the contemplation of that very profound companionship which God so loved from eternity and which he gave even to his son, and in which I too was wont to find my joy; namely in the poverty, the pain, and the disgrace of the Son of the living God was my wonted rest and the bed on which I lay. And even from that whole manner of beholding God in darkness, which so greatly gladdened me, I am expelled. And I left all that earlier state with such great consecration and satisfaction that I can in no way imagine it; I recall only that I no longer have it.

And in these unspeakable goods and workings that occur in my soul, God first shows himself in the soul and works the unspeakable. Then he reveals himself and opens himself to the soul and grants her still greater gifts with still greater certainty and in nameless clarity.

At first, however, he shows himself to the soul in twofold manner. In the one manner he represents himself inwardly in my soul, and then I see him as present and recognize how he is present in all nature and in everything that has existence—in the demon, in the good angel, in hell, in paradise, in adultery, in murder, in every good work, and in everything that has existence in any way, in the beautiful and in the ugly. Therefore during the time I am in this truth I rejoice equally when I see God or an angel or a good work or even an evil work; and in this manner God very often represents himself in my soul. And this representation of himself, or this presence, is an illumination with great truth and with divine grace; so that the soul, when it sees this, cannot take offense at anything. . . .

In another manner God represents himself in a more particular way, different from the first, and gives another joy, and gathers the entire soul into himself, and works a great thing in the soul with far mightier mercy and with the unnameable abyss of joys and radiations, so that this self-display of God without other gifts is that good which the saints have in eternal life. And although I am not worthy to speak of it—indeed my speaking is more a devastation and a blasphemy than any sort of imparting—yet I say that in this there are expansions of the soul, whereby the soul becomes more capable of grasping and having God.

And immediately after God has shown himself to the soul, he reveals himself and opens himself to her and expands the soul and gives her the gifts and the sweets that she never experienced before, and with far greater depth than I have said. And then the soul is drawn out of all darkness, and is given a greater recognition of God than I can understand the possibility of, and that with so great a brightness and with so great a sweetness and certainty and in so deep an abyss that there is no heart that could attain this. Therefore my heart, too, cannot arrive afterward at an understanding of any of this, nor a thought of any of this; only this one thing—that it is a gift from God to the soul, that she might be exalted therein, but that otherwise no heart could extend itself so far. And therefore the soul cannot say anything about it at all, nor can any word be found that would say or sound it, nor can any thought or any understanding expand itself to these things: They are so vastly beyond everything, in this and in every other sense, that God cannot be conveyed by anything that can be said or thought. . . .

And although from without I can receive some small measure of sorrows and joys, yet there is within my soul a chamber in which no joy or sorrow or enjoyment of any virtue or of any nameable thing enters; the only thing that enters is that sole good. And in this revelation of God (although I blaspheme when I name Christ so, for I cannot completely designate him with any word) is the whole truth. And in him I recognize and possess the whole truth that is in heaven and on earth and in hell and in every creature, with so great a reality and with so great a certainty that I could in no way believe anything else, even if the whole world were to testify to the contrary, and even mock it. For I see him who is Being; and how he is the being of all created natures. And I see how he has made me capable of understanding all these things better than I did before, when I saw him in that darkness which used to make me so glad. And I see myself alone with God, wholly pure, wholly sanctified, wholly true, wholly honest, wholly confirmed, wholly heavenly in him, and when I am in this state, I am no longer mindful of any other thing. And once, when I was in this state, God spoke to me: "Daughter of divine wisdom, temple of the beloved, bliss of the beloved and daughter of peace, in you rests the whole Trinity, the whole truth, so that you possess me and I possess you." . . .

Yet to this state I did not advance, but I was led and exalted by God, so that I did not know how to wish for this state or to desire it or to strive for it, and now I am constantly in it. And very often my soul is exalted by God, and my consent is not asked. For when I do not expect it or think of it my soul is suddenly exalted by God the Lord, and I embrace the whole world, and it seems to me that I am not on earth, but am standing in heaven, in God. And this exalted state in which I now am is above the others that I possessed hitherto, for it is of such great fullness and such great clarity and certainty and ennoblement and expansion that I feel no other state approaches it. And this revelation of God I have had more than a thousand times; always new and always in a different manner.

CATHERINE OF SIENA (1347–1380)

From the notes of Raimund of Capua, her confessor

Once when she lay upon her bed, burdened with many pains, and desired to speak with me of certain things which the Lord had revealed to her, she summoned me in secret. And when I had come to her and stood at her bedside, she began, though feverish, to speak in her usual way of God and to tell of the things that had been revealed to her that day. But when I heard such great and unheard-of things, I said in my heart, forgetful of the grace previously received and ungrateful for it, "Do you suppose that all the things she says are true?" And while I thought thus and turned toward her who was speaking, her face was changed in an instant into the face of a bearded man who, gazing at me with staring eyes, gave me a great fright. And the face was rather long, of middle age, and had a beard that was not long, the color of wheat, and in appearance it displayed such majesty that it thereby revealed itself as the Savior. Moreover, at that time I could not distinguish any other face than this. And when I raised my hands to my shoulders in consternation and terror, crying out, "Who is this who is gazing at me?" the virgin answered, "He who is." When this was said, this face disappeared suddenly, and I saw clearly the features of the virgin, which I had previously been unable to distinguish.

Once when she was praying with great fervor, saying with the prophet, "Create in me a clean heart, O God, and renew a right spirit within me," and particularly begging God to take from her her own heart and her own will, he himself consoled her with this vision. It seemed to her that the eternal bridegroom was coming to her in his usual manner, opening her left side, taking out her heart and departing from her, and she was left without any heart at all. This vision was so persistent and so detrimental to the feeling of the flesh that she told her confessor in confession that she no longer had a heart in her breast; and when he made a jest concerning that word and, jesting, rebuked her in a certain way, she repeated what she had said and confirmed it, saying, "In truth, Father, as far as I can judge by bodily feeling, I think that I am indeed without a heart, for the Lord appeared to me, opened my left side, took out my heart and departed." And when he replied that it was impossible to live without a heart, the virgin of the Lord declared that with God nothing is impossible, and she believed with certainty that she was robbed of her heart. And thus for many days she repeated the same, saying that she lived without a heart.

One day she remained in prayer after the departure of the others in the chapel of the brothers of the preaching order in Siena, where the sisters used to gather. When she arose upon waking from the sleep of her usual detachment, a light of heaven suddenly shone round about her, and in the light the Lord appeared to her, bearing in his consecrated hands a reddish and shining human heart. And when, at the arrival of him who was the cause of the light, she sank trembling to the ground, the Lord approached her, opened her left side once more, placed inside her that heart which he bore in his hands, and said, "See, beloved daughter, just as I took your heart from you the other day, so I am now giving you my heart, with which you will live from now on."

CATHERINE OF GENOA (1447–1510)

The pure and clear love can desire nothing of God, however good it may be, that could be called participation, for it wants God himself, pure, clear, and great as he is; and if the tiniest point were missing, this love could not be satisfied, but indeed would deem itself in hell. Therefore I say that I want no created love, no love that one can taste, grasp, or enjoy. I do not want, I say, a love that passes through the understanding, through the memory, through the will; for pure love transcends all things and strides over them and says, "I will not be content until I am locked and enclosed within that divine bosom in which all created forms lose themselves and, so lost, remain divine." And in no other way can the pure, true, and clear love be contented.

Therefore I have resolved that as long as I live I will say to the world, "Outwardly do with me what you will, but inwardly leave me; for I cannot and do not desire and do not wish to be able to desire to be occupied save in God alone, who has taken my inner being and has so enclosed it in himself that he will not open it to anyone. Know that he does nothing else but to consume this humanity, his creature, within and without; and when it is entirely consumed in him, both will go out of this body and ascend, united, into our homeland. I can therefore see nothing within except him, for he does not let anyone else in, and myself even less than the others, for I am more his enemy."

And when I am nonetheless forced to mention this I, for the sake of the life of the world, which does not know how to speak in any other way—that is, when I mention myself or am mentioned by others—then I say in myself, "My I is God, and I know no other I than this my God." I say the same thing when I speak of being. Every thing that has being has it from God's highest essence through participation; but the pure and clear love cannot be content with seeing that it has acquired God through participation, nor with his being in it as a creature, as he is in other creatures that participate in God, some more, some less. This love cannot bear such comparison, but says with great enamored force, "My being is God, not through participation, but through true transformation and through annihilation of my own being." . . .

So in God is my being, my I, my strength, my bliss, my desire. But this I that I often call so—I do it because I cannot speak otherwise, but in truth I no longer know what the I is, or the Mine, or desire, or the good, or bliss. I can no longer turn my eyes on anything, wherever it be, in heaven or on earth. And if I nevertheless say a few words that have in themselves the form of humility or spirituality, in my innermost being I know and feel nothing of it; indeed, I am disconcerted that I speak so many words that are so different from the truth and from what I feel.

I do not want a love that would be for God or in God. I cannot bear to see this word *for,* this word *in,* for to me they indicate a thing that would be between me and God. But the pure and clear love cannot bear this, and this purity and clarity is as great as God himself is in order to be his own.

I find in myself by the grace of God a satisfaction without nourishment, a love without fear; that is, fear that it could ever be taken from me. Faith seems to me wholly lost, and hope dead; for it seems to me that I have and hold in certainty that which I believed and hoped at other times. I no longer see union, for I know nothing more and can see nothing more than him alone without me. I do not know where the I is, nor do I seek it, nor do I wish to know or be cognizant of it. I am so plunged and submerged in the source of his infinite love, as if I were quite under water in the sea and could not touch, see, feel anything on any side except water. I am so submerged in the sweet fire of love that I cannot grasp anything except the whole of love, which melts all the marrow of my soul and body. And sometimes I feel as if my body were made entirely of some yielding substance; and I can no longer bear my body, because of the estrangement in which I stand to bodily things.

Therefore it seems to me that I am no longer of this world, since I can no longer do the work of the world like the others; indeed, every action of others that I see disturbs me, for I do not work as they do, nor as I myself used to do. I feel myself altogether estranged from earthly affairs, and from my own most of all, so that I cannot endure even to see them. And I say to everything, "Let me go, for I can no longer care for you or remember you; rather it is as if you did not exist for me. I cannot work, or walk, or stand, or speak, but all this seems to me a useless thing, superfluous to the world." Many are astonished at this, and since they do not know the reason, they are offended. And truly, if it were not that God stands by me, the world would often consider me mad, and that is because I almost always live outside myself.

God became man in order to make me God; therefore I want to be changed completely into pure God.

MARIA MADDALENA DE' PAZZI (1566–1607)

Besides the constant fervor which made her heart melt and made her constantly think of God, speak of God, work for God, and which often bereft her of her senses and placed her wholly in God, she sometimes came into such great ardor that it could no longer be enclosed within her breast, but poured out over her face, into her actions, and broke forth in her words. She, who because of her penitential exercises was generally weak, sickly, pale, and wasted, regained her full strength when she was surprised by these flames of love, and her face became full and glowing, her eyes like two shining stars, and her glance serene and glad as that of a blessed angel. She found no rest, and could not remain in one place. In order to pour out this ardor which she could not hold in herself, she was forced to bestir herself and move about in a wondrous manner. Therefore during these outbreaks she would be seen running swiftly from place to place; as if raving with love she went through the convent, calling in a loud voice, "Love, love, love!" And when she could not bear so great a fire of love, she said, "O my Lord, no more love, no more love." . . . To the sisters who followed her she said, "You do not know, dear sisters, that my Jesus is nothing else but love, he is mad with love. I say you are mad with love, my Jesus, and I will always say it. You are altogether lovely and merry, you refresh and console, you nourish and unite, you are torment and relief, effort and rest, death and life in one.

What is not in you? You are wise and willful, sublime and immeasurable, wonderful and inexpressible."

At other times she burned with desire that this loving God should be recognized and revered by humankind, and then, turned toward heaven, she would say, "O love, O love! Give me so strong a voice, O my Lord, so that, when it calls you love, it may be heard from the East to the West and by all parts of the earth even into hell, so that you may be recognized and revered as the true love. O love, you penetrate and pierce, you tear and bind, you rule all things; you are heaven and earth, fire and air, blood and water; you are God and man."

Stripping the ornaments from an image of the child Jesus, she said, "I want you naked, O my Jesus, for I could not bear you in the infinity of your virtues and perfections; I want your naked, naked humanity."

FROM HER COMMUNICATIONS

I saw that Jesus united with his bride in the closest union, laid his head upon the head of his bride, his eyes on hers, his mouth, his hands, his feet, all his limbs on hers, so that the bride became one with him and wanted all that the bridegroom wanted, saw everything that the bridegroom saw, tasted everything that the bridegroom tasted. And God wants nothing else than that the soul should unite herself to him in this manner and that he should be entirely united with her. And when the soul leans her head against Jesus' head, she can want nothing save to unite with God, and that God should unite with her. God sees himself in her wholly, and out of himself alone he is capable of himself and sees himself in all creatures, even in those that have no sensation, and in them through the power by which he gives them being and makes them act and bear fruit. Thus the soul, when its eyes are upon Jesus' eyes, sees itself in God and God in all things.

After the most holy communion I contemplated the great union of the soul with God through the sacrament, and in an instant I saw myself wholly united with God, transformed into God, and outside all bodily feeling, so that I would have felt nothing if I had been thrown into a fiery furnace. I did not know whether I was dead or alive, in the body or in the soul, on earth or in heaven; I saw only the whole glorious God in himself, loving himself purely, knowing himself infinitely, embracing all created things in pure infinite love, a oneness in three, an undivided Trinity, a God of boundless love, all-exalted in goodness, incomprehensible and unfathomable; so that I was with him and found nothing more of myself; only this I saw, that I am in God; but I did not see myself, only God alone.

The Spanish Women

TERESA DE JESUS (1515–1582)

LETTER TO HER CONFESSOR, FATHER RODRIGO ALVAREZ

It is so hard to speak of inner things—and still harder to do this in such a way that they may be understood, particularly when one must be brief—that, unless obedience brings it about, it is a difficult thing to get it right, especially with such difficult subjects. But it will not do much harm if I write absurdities, since this is destined for hands that have no doubt received even greater follies from me in the past. In all that I say I pray your grace to consider that I by no means intend to suppose that I have got it right; for possibly I myself would not understand it. But I can assure you that I will not say anything that I myself have not experienced several times or many times. Whether it is good or not, may your grace judge and let me know. . . .

The first, as it seems to me, supernatural prayer that I noticed in myself . . . is an inward concentration which is so felt in the soul that it seems to her that she has other senses than the outward ones and as if she wished to withdraw from the hubbub of the outward senses. Sometimes it draws her so much after it that she feels the impulse to close her eyes and to see nothing, hear nothing, understand nothing, except that with which the soul is just then occupied, that is, her dealings with God alone. No sense is lost here, no faculty; everything remains intact, but only for the purpose of conversing with God. Those to whom such things have been given will easily understand this, but not those to whom it has not happened; at least, with such a person one must use many words and comparisons.

This concentration often produces a calmness and inner peace, in which the soul finds that there is nothing left for her to do; even speech is burdensome to her. I mean the recitation of the prayer and reflective contemplation; she wants nothing but love. This lasts a while, and a good while.

From this prayer there usually comes a sleep which is called the sleep of the faculties, though they are neither so deadened nor so suspended that one could call this sleep a trance; nor is it a unification.

Sometimes—quite often—the soul perceives that her will alone is unified and recognizes very clearly (so it seems to me at least) that it is completely occupied in God. At the same time the soul feels the impossibility of being anything else and doing anything else. Both other faculties of the soul are free for all occupations and exercises in the service of God. . . .

When a unification of all the soul's faculties takes place, it is quite different; for then they cannot act in any matter, reason being as if suspended. The will loves more than it understands; but it does not even understand whether it loves, nor what it does, so as to be able to say it. Memory, it seems to me, is not present here at all, nor thought, and the senses are not awake, but it is as if one had lost them—as it seems to me, in order that the soul may be more thoroughly occupied with what she enjoys. This state loses itself in a short time and is soon over. . . .

Trance and exaltation are, I think, the same thing. . . . The only difference between it and the trance is that the trance lasts longer and is outwardly more perceptible. The breath is so shortened that one cannot speak, nor open one's eyes . . . When the trance is great, the hands become ice-cold and sometimes extend straight out, like bars, and the body remains in the position it had when the trance seized it, on its feet or kneeling. The soul at such times stands so much in the enjoyment of what the Lord is showing to her that it is as if she forgot to animate the body and left it, helpless, behind. If this state continues for a longer time, a feeling of it remains in the limbs. . . .

The difference between trance and abduction is that in trance the soul gradually dies to outward things, loses the senses and lives for God; abduction, on the other hand, sets in with a single recognition which God gives to the innermost part of the soul with such swiftness that it seems as if the soul's higher part were being snatched away; the soul imagines that this higher part is detaching itself from the body. And at the beginning she needs courage in order to throw herself into the arms of the Lord, so that he may lift her up whithersoever he will. For as long as God does not set the soul in the peace to which he wishes to raise her—to raise her, I say, in order that she may apprehend lofty things—she must truly be resolved at first to die for him; for the poor soul does not know what is to come of this. . . .

Spiritual flight is something which I do not know how to name and which arises from the inner ground of the soul. . . . It seems to me as if soul and spirit must be one nature. Somewhat like a fire that is to become great and has everything ready for burning, so the soul with her readiness for God resembles a fire: It ignites swiftly, throws out a flame, and blazes up, although the fire in its being is below and does not cease to be a fire by the flame's climbing upward. Thus it occurs to the soul, which so quickly brings forth something, and moreover something so precious, which ascends to the upper spheres and arrives where God will have it. It appears in truth as a flight. I know no other more suitable comparison; I know only that one perceives spiritual flight very distinctly, and that one cannot prevent it.

It seems as if that little bird, the spirit, takes wing from this misery of the flesh, this prison of the body, in order that, once free of it, it may surrender itself the more to what the Lord grants to it. It is such a delicate, fine, precious matter, insofar as the soul can understand it, that it seems to her as if no deception could prevail in it, nor in any of these matters. Once the state has passed, there remains an anxiety because the one who received is so insignificant that she thinks she has every reason to fear; although in the inner part of the soul certainty and confidence remain. . . .

The onset I call a desire, which comes over the soul at times, without being preceded by a prayer; for the most part there is also a sudden knowledge that God is not here and that no word which the soul hears goes to him. This knowledge is sometimes so mighty and so powerful that it drives one out of one's mind in an instant, as when painful news or a great surprise is suddenly imparted to a person, or other things of this nature that deprive thought of reflection that might console it, so that it is as if stunned. So it is here too, only that the pain comes from such a matter that the soul knows that death is appropriate for its sake. This is why everything the soul receives now causes her greater torment, as if the Lord wanted only this, that her entire being should be good for nothing else and that she should receive no consolation nor remember that it is God's will for her to live. Rather she supposes herself to be in an indescribable state of solitude and abandonment by all; for the whole world and everything in it causes her pain, and it seems to her as if no creature wants to keep her company.

The soul desires nothing save her creator; she recognizes now how impossible this is without her death; but since she is not allowed to kill herself, she dies of longing for death, in such a manner that in truth there is danger of death in it. She sees herself as it were suspended between heaven and earth and does not know what to do with herself. From time to time God gives her some knowledge of himself, so that she may become aware of what she lacks; this occurs in so strange a manner that one cannot say it, nor describe the torment, for there is no torment on earth, at least among those I have endured, that can equal it. If it lasts only half an hour, the body is so wrenched from its connections, and all the bones are so torn apart, that the hands no longer have sufficient strength for writing. . . .

Of all this the soul feels nothing until that onset is over. Then she has enough to do to feel it inwardly, and I believe that she would not notice severe tortures. Yet she has all her wits and can speak and look, but not walk, because the great blow of love has thrown her down. . . . The soul knows that it is a great grace of God; but if it lasted, life could not endure. . . . Another form of prayer is like a wounding that truly seems to the soul as if an arrow pierced her through the heart, in her deepest self. This awakens a great pain, which breaks out in lamentation, yet is so sweet that the soul would never wish to be deprived of it. This pain is not a sensation of the senses, nor is the wound to be understood as a bodily wound, for only in the inner part of the soul is the impression appearing, without any suffering of the body. But since it can be communicated only by comparisons, they come out clumsy, only I do not know any other way of saying it. Such things can neither be said nor written; for no one can understand them except one who has experienced them; I mean, how deeply the pain penetrates. At other times it seems as if this wound of love calls forth from the soul's inner ground the great movements which she can in no way produce if the Lord does not give them, and which she cannot resist when it is his will to give them to her. These movements are such lively and tender wishes for God that one cannot express them; but since the soul sees itself in chains, so that she cannot enjoy God as she would like, she acquires a great horror of the body. It seems to the soul like a high wall that prevents her from enjoying what she would already have enjoyed in herself before this time, if it were not for the obstacle of the body.

LETTER TO PETER OF ALCANTARA

My present manner of prayer is as follows: While praying I am seldom able to reflect with my reason, for the soul immediately begins to concentrate itself and arrive at peacefulness or a trance, so that it cannot use the senses at all, except perhaps for hearing, and even that is useless for hearing anything else.

It often happens that without wishing to think about God in any way, even while pondering over quite different matters, and thinking that however hard I tried I would not be able to pray because I am in such a state of aridity, to which bodily pains contribute, I am caught up so suddenly by concentration and spiritual exaltation that I cannot preserve myself. But a moment suffices to produce the effects and the gain that come of it. This occurs without my seeing a vision or intending anything or knowing where I am; my soul merely seems to lose itself. At the same time, however, I see it in possession of such great gain that if I were to devote a year to acquiring this, I could not possibly succeed.

At other times I am attacked so mightily by a dissolving before God that I cannot preserve myself. It seems to me as if my life wants to flow away, and so I feel driven to cry aloud and to call on God. This attacks me with great force. Sometimes I cannot sit still, such great fears are put into me. This torment comes to me without my seeking after it, but it is of such kind that the soul would like never to come out of it as long as she lives. These fears concern the will to live no longer: It seems to us as though one could receive no help in life, so that death is the means of seeing God, but one is not allowed to choose death. Therefore it appears to my soul that all are well comforted, except her, and as if all found help in their affliction, except her. This creates such distress that if God did not grant help with a trance in which all is calmed and the soul comes into great peace and great contentment, it would be impossible to free oneself of this torment.

At still other times I am seized by a desire to serve God, which attacks me so violently that I cannot represent it as great enough; this is accompanied by pain over the perception of how little use I am. Then it seems to me that nothing could happen to me—no hardship, no death, no torture—that I would not bear with ease. This also occurs without reflection in an instant in which I am completely transformed, without knowing from whence I draw such strength. It seems to me that I must call out loud and let everyone know how necessary it is for them not to be content with little, and how great is the good that God will give us if we prepare ourselves to receive it. I say that that desire is so violent that I am destroying myself within myself. It seems to me then that I desire what is not possible for me. It seems to me that I am bound to this body in order that I may be unable to serve God and my order in any way whatsoever. For if I were not in the body, I would accomplish uncommon things, as far as my faculties permitted. But because I now see how I am quite without any power to serve God, I feel this pain so greatly that I cannot describe it. But at last I obtain the gift: the comfort of God.

ANNA GARCIAS (ANNA A SAN BARTOLOMEO) (1549–1626)

I once saw my soul fashioned like a little silkworm, which has been diligently fed and carefully kept by those who raised it. But when it is grown it begins to spin with its little snout a delicate little silken thread to make a little hut for itself, and in so doing it enjoys such sweetness that it does not notice its own dying until, robbed of all its powers, it remains enclosed and dead in its shell. Now my soul saw something similar in itself, for with just such sweetness and quiet it gave the Almighty God everything it had in itself and enclosed itself like a little silkworm in its nonbeing and in the recognition of its nothingness, with a sweet love that spins at all times in my heart, which no longer wishes to be or to live, for dying is the true being of the soul.

The Seventeenth Century in France

ARMELLE NICOLAS (1606–1671)

I regarded myself as a poor malefactor who desires to enter into a friendship with her prince. . . . The more wretched I saw myself, the more I wished to unite myself with him whom I knew as my only good and my all.

Thus I passed the entire Lenten season. On Good Friday I went to hear the sermon. Before I had heard the sufferings of my Savior spoken of for a quarter of an hour, my heart was already so powerfully wrenched and pierced by sorrows that I could no longer remain, but was forced to leave for fear that my heart would break in pieces, or at least reveal by some action how violently it was moved. I went home; there was no one there at the time. I locked myself in; and at first I ran from one place to another and screamed till I was out of breath, like a madwoman and one who is quite beside herself; afterward I threw myself down on the floor and screamed, "Mercy, Lord, mercy!" I begged the whole host of heaven for aid and conjured all the saints to help me. And turning to God, I said to him with flaming ardor, "O my Lord and my God, see, the day has come when I must be all yours. Cleanse and wash me in your dear blood. Anoint my heart with the oil of your mercy. Pierce me with the arrows of your holy love. Accept me into the ranks of your disciples. Show yourself to me and unite with me."

In the middle of this prayer, while I was saying just these words, which were inwardly dictated to me—for I myself did not know what I was saying and did not even understand the meaning of these words, nor yet the mysteries they contain, only I was forced and compelled to speak them; and this I did with a forceful violence, so that it seemed to me that every word was an arrow, well sharpened to penetrate into God's very heart—as I lay in the midst of this prayer and had labored and tormented myself, suddenly in an instant I was led up to the highest attic of the house, without knowing how; I simply found myself there, although beforehand I had no thought of it.

Then I threw myself down on the floor, because I could no longer hold or carry myself, so extreme was the distress to which I had been brought. And in the same moment God let a ray of his divine light shine into the depth of my heart; through this ray he revealed himself to me and let me know clearly that he whom I had so desired was entering into me and taking full possession of me. When this grace occurred to me, I felt myself wholly clothed and surrounded as with a light. In the beginning terror came over me, but it lasted only a moment, for immediately my heart was again placed in surety and so changed that I no longer knew myself, and I felt such a contentment of all desires that I did not know whether I was on earth or in heaven. I remained for some time motionless as a statue, so that I could not move. And from this time on all the faculties of my soul were so fulfilled and contented, and in all my senses was such a great peace, that I could in no way doubt that God had now intimately united himself with me, as had been my fervent wish up till then. And this truth was as infallibly certain in me as if I had seen it with my own eyes, for the light that was then communicated to me far surpassed all that may be seen with the eyes.

All my good is God alone, and now that he is all mine through his great mercy and kindness, just as I am all his, it is no longer necessary for me to strive to acquire something. I have nothing further to do but to rest in the good that is his; as he rests in me, I also rest in him, because I am entirely enclosed and annihilated in him. There I no longer find myself, and when I say, "I enjoy, I love, I possess," it is no longer I who receives this; but rather his love is my love, his riches are my riches, his peace is my rest, his ways are my pleasure, and so it is with all his divine perfections. Now there is nothing more that I could desire, for I am quite overwhelmed with good things, nor must I fear to lose them, for they belong to him alone, my love and my all. But I no longer possess them as my own, and thus I do not have to fear that they might be taken from me.

Now God is everything, but I am no more; by his mercy I have come to the place whence I came forth. He alone, and no longer I myself, lives and rules in me, for I am no longer in myself, but in him, where I no longer find myself, and where I have lost myself. It is he alone who gives himself life, for I now see nothing more that is not he himself.

O love and infinite goodness, I can no longer flee from you! You run ahead of me everywhere, and I find you everywhere. Now I no longer see you through clouds, I see you quite clearly and openly, without cover or curtain. Now there is no longer anything mediating between you and me. What do you want me to do, and how shall I be able to go on living on earth with this brightness and this divine fire that consumes me? I have never found myself in such a state. The inordinate might that I feel exceeds all that is extraordinary, and I no longer know whither I am to turn, what I am to say, only this: that love everywhere leads me out of myself and overcomes me everywhere.

Since the feast of my holy Mother I have seen my soul detached from all things, so pure, so solitary, so secluded, that it seems as if it no longer lives in my body, which, as it seems to me, seeks nothing except to follow the soul as if without feeling. I no longer have any thoughts or anything else that could detain or occupy me, as otherwise generally happens. The nature and the unfathomability of God is the only object that penetrates and consumes my soul in an incomprehensible way, and by thus consuming it, widens it out, so that I know of no goal or end to it. Formerly I wanted to do everything and undertake everything, but now it is quite otherwise with me, for nothing approaches me anymore. I understand everything and am understood by nothing. My soul is solitary, simple and pure, and when I see it so, I see a miracle. If this lasts much longer in me, I think I shall die of it. Outwardly I go about my work as usual, without losing this contemplation, but my God takes it from me sometimes and allows a few thoughts to come into my mind and distract me from it; otherwise I would have died before now. No one can express, no one can understand the love that consumes me. It is infinite and yet grows more and more each day.

ANTOINETTE BOURIGNON (1616–1680)

FROM A LETTER

To answer the inquiry you have repeatedly addressed to me, as to how I perceive God and speak with him, I will simply say what I can say.

God is spirit, the soul is spirit; they communicate themselves to each other in the spirit—not by words of language, but by spiritual communications, which however are more understandable than the most skillful eloquence in the world.

God makes himself known to the soul through inner movements which the soul perceives and understands to the extent that it is free from earthly ideas; and the more the soul's faculties cease, the more understandable God's movements are to the soul.

God's communications are infallible when the soul is empty of all images and stands in the forgetfulness of all created things; but they are dubious when the soul is working through imaginations and is seeking sentimentalities or anything else that is not God, bare of all else. Even the saints have committed spiritual vanities in this point through visions, voices, ecstasies, and other sentimentalities to which the imagination contributes.

God is pure spirit; the purified soul transforms itself into him and needs no words and no looks to perceive him, any more than we need the eye or the tongue in order to perceive our own idea. . . .

I am a pure nothing; but God is everything in me. He teaches me, he works, he speaks in me, without nature contributing more than the mere tool, as a brush contributes to the art of a beautiful painting.

JEANNE MARIE BOUVIERES DE LA MOTHE GUYON (1648–1717)

Such a soul receives everything from the ground, directly; and from there it pours out upon the faculties and the senses, as God pleases. It is not thus with other souls, who receive indirectly: There what is received falls into the faculties, and from there it unites with the center. But in the first-mentioned souls it discharges itself from the center onto the faculties and the senses. They let everything pass by, and nothing makes an impression on their spirit or their heart. Moreover, to them the things they experience do not seem like extraordinary things, prophecies and such, the way they appear to the others; one says them quite naturally, without knowing what one is saying or why one is saying it; without anything extraordinary. One says and writes what one does not know; and in saying and writing it one sees that these are things one has never thought of. It is like a person who possesses in her ground an inexhaustible treasure, without ever thinking of her possession; she does not know her own riches, she does not see them; but in this ground she finds, whenever necessary, everything she needs. Past, present, and future are there in the manner of a present and eternal moment, not as prophecy, which regards the future as a thing that is to come, but as everything is seen in the present in the eternal moment, in God himself; without knowing how one sees or knows it; with a sure fidelity in the saying of the things as they are given, without intention and without looking back; without considering whether one speaks of the future or the present; without troubling oneself over whether these things are fulfilled or not, in one way or the other, whether they have one meaning or another. From this ground, so lost, these wonders proceed.

When my spirit had been enlightened, my soul was placed in an infinite wideness. I recognized the difference between the gifts of grace that had preceded this state and those that followed it. Before it, everything gathered and was bound together within, and I possessed God in my ground and in the secrecy of my soul; but then I was possessed by him, in such a wide, pure, and infinite way that there is nothing similar. Once God was as if enclosed in me, and I was united with him in my ground; but then I was as if sunk in the sea. Formerly thoughts and intentions did become lost; but in however inconspicuous a way, the soul let them drop, and that is still a doing; but then they had disappeared, and in so naked, so pure, so lost a manner that the soul has no doing of its own, however simple and delicate; at least none that could come to its notice. . . .

This wideness, which is not limited by any thing, however simple, grows with each day, so that it seems that the soul, which participates in the qualities of her bridegroom, participates above all in his infinity. Once, one was as if drawn inward and enclosed; then I felt that a hand, far stronger than the first, drew me out of myself and sunk me without look, without light, without knowledge in God.

In the beginning of the new life I saw clearly that the soul is united with its God without means or intermediary; but it was not yet completely lost. It lost itself with every day in him, the way one sees a river that loses itself in the ocean first pour into the ocean, then dissolve in it, so that the river is distinct from the sea for some time, until at last it gradually changes itself into the sea itself, which, slowly imparting its qualities to the stream, changes it so much into itself that soon it is all one sea. I have gradually experienced the same thing with my soul, as God gradually loses it in himself, draws it out of its selfhood and imparts his selfhood to it.

The senses are like children that wander and run around; but they do not confuse this ground without ground, which is entirely lost, entirely bare, and which is no longer hindered by anything, just as it is no longer supported by anything.

My prayer was always the same: not a prayer in me, but in God, very simple, very pure, and very clear. It is no longer a prayer but a state of which I can say nothing because of its great purity. I do not believe that there can be anything simpler or more unified in the world. It is a state of which one can say nothing because it surpasses all expression; a state in which the creature is so completely lost and sunk that though it may be outwardly free, inwardly it no longer possesses anything. Thus its happiness is also immutable. Everything is God, and the soul becomes aware of nothing but God. It has no more perfection to desire, has no more striving, no interval, no union; everything is consummated in unity, but in such a free, light, natural way that the soul lives in God and from God, as naturally as the body lives by the air it breathes.

ELIE MARION

FROM A STATEMENT BY MARION, THE CAMISARD LEADER, IN
JANUARY 1707

On the first day of the year 1703, when we, the family and a few
relations, had gone apart in order to spend part of the day in
prayer and other pious exercises, one of my brothers received an
inspiration; and a few moments afterward I suddenly felt a great
warmth, which seized my heart and gradually spread through my
whole body. I also found myself a little oppressed, and this forced
me to heave great sighs; yet I kept them back as well as I could,
for the sake of the company. A few moments later a power I could
no longer resist took full possession of me and made me burst out
into great shrieks that were interrupted by deep sobbing, and my
eyes shed rivulets of tears. I was violently struck by a fearful conception of my sins, which appeared to me black, ghastly, and infinite in number. I felt them like a burden that bent my head down-
ward, and the more they loaded themselves on me, the stronger
my screaming and weeping became. They filled my spirit with
terror; and in my fear I could neither speak nor pray to God.
Nevertheless I felt something good and blessed that did not permit
my terror to turn into murmuring or despair. My God struck me
and encouraged me at the same time. Then my brother fell into
a second trance and said in a loud voice that it was my sins that
were making me suffer. And at the same time he began to recite
a long enumeration of these sins and to describe them before all
the people who were there, as if he had seen them or had read in
my heart; I myself could not have given a more faithful picture of
my own state.

When he had finished this dreadful portrayal, without forgetting
anything and with emphasis on the sins that troubled my spirit the
most, I felt greatly relieved. When thus some calm had come, my
burden also became lighter, and I greatly enjoyed the freedom that
was returned to me, to lift my heart and my voice to God. I used
this fortunate time and did not cease to plead for the mercy of my
heavenly Father, which by his infinite compassion spoke to my
heart of peace and dried the tears from my eyes. I had a restful
night; but on waking I fell into movements similar to those which

from that time until now have always seized me while in trance and which were accompanied by very frequent sobbing. This happened to me three or four times a day, for three weeks or a month; and God put it into my heart to use this time for fasting and prayer. The further I progressed, the more my consolation increased, and finally, may my God be praised for it, I entered into the possession of this blissful contentment of the spirit, which is a great gain.

I found myself quite transformed. The things that had been most pleasant to me before my Creator made me a new heart became repulsive, even unbearable, to me. And at last it was a new joy for my soul when after a month of mute trances, if I may call it thus, it pleased God to loosen my tongue and to place his word in my mouth. As his Holy Spirit had moved my body in order to waken it out of its rigidity and to throw down its haughtiness, so it was also his will to move my tongue and my lips and to employ these feeble organs according to his pleasure. I will not attempt to express what my astonishment and joy were when I heard a brook of holy words flowing through my mouth, whose originator was not my spirit, and which gladdened my ears.

In the first inspiration God sent me when he loosened my tongue, his Holy Spirit spoke to me in these words: "I assure you, my child, that from your mother's womb I have destined you for my honor." Blessed words, which until the last sigh of my life will be engraved on my heart. This same spirit of wisdom and grace also declared to me that it was necessary for me to take up weapons that I might join my brothers who had been bravely fighting in God's cause for about six months. I therefore left my father's house at the beginning of February and went to join a troup of Christian soldiers, whom I subsequently had the honor of commanding.

The Seventeenth Century in Germany and the Netherlands

JAKOB BÖHME (1575–1624)

But when in such gloom I raised up my spirit, understanding little or nothing of what that spirit was, and lifted it up in God earnestly, as in a great storm, and my whole heart and emotional being, along with all other thoughts and will, locked themselves into it, without ceasing to wrestle with God's love and mercy, and without letting go unless he bless me, that is, enlighten me with his Holy Spirit, that I might understand his will and be rid of my sadness—then the spirit broke through.

But when in my determined zeal I stormed thus hard against God and the gates of all hells, as if I had still more strength, willing to stake my life on it, which to be sure would not have been in my power had the spirit of God not sustained me forthwith—after certain hard storms my spirit broke through the gates of hell into the inmost birth of the Godhead and was embraced there with love, as a bridegroom embraces his dear bride.

But what triumphing there was in the spirit, I cannot write or say, nor can it be compared with anything, except where in the midst of death life is born; it may be compared to the resurrection of the dead.

In this light my spirit forthwith saw through everything, and by every creature, even plants and grass, it recognized God—who he is, and what he is, and what is his will.

A PAGE (anonymous, ca. 1596)

After four weeks the sweet angel of my consolation again appeared to me and spoke much to me of the beauty of the children of God and made me wish heartily that I might see them in their splendid majesty. To him I said, "O my darling angel, my sweet little brother, please take me once more to the hall of high heaven, to the beautiful children of God, that I may see their countenance in justice." And he took me up and led me to heaven, where I had been four weeks previously, and set me in the midst of the children of God, who were all gathered there. But I did not see the Lord God sitting on his golden throne. So I said, "Where is the Lord God, my most dear father?"

He said, "He is in his children. See, God's truth is in his children. For his sons and his daughters are his temples in which he dwells and which he has filled with his glory."

And I looked around for the thousand times a thousand children of God and became aware that they were shining from the inner truth of God like bright clear suns. There I saw living sapphires and rubies. The light of the Lord sparkled in their bodies and drove them so that they could not stand still, for the clarity of the Lord is a living clarity. But they were held by the angel of God, so that they could not flee whither they wanted to go, for their time was not yet come.

Then one of the highest angels said, "You are all full of the living spirit. That is your honor, against the dishonor of the world. Then suffer therefore, and console yourselves with this great splendor."

But in me such a light blazed up from the clarity of the Lord that I could see into the middle of God's heart and could well recognize his great love and his heavenly counsel concerning me. Though I did not see him outwardly, I recognized him inwardly, for his light was in me, and I became full of the joy of God, so that I almost died of it. For where the Lord God is, there is his wisdom and joy.

But soon afterward I was given a thorn in the flesh, that is, great sorrow in my heart, that I might not exalt myself on account of such great splendor, nor misuse it for security. And every enlightened one, along with me, returned to his place and his misery until the day that will bring them back.

HANS ENGELBRECHT (1599–1642)

When I lay thus struggling in agony, death struck me after a while, starting from my feet; and I lay and died from my feet upwards; it took me twelve hours to die thus, having neither eaten nor drunk for about a week. Having lain down and become ill on Friday, I died on Thursday, about a week later. On Thursday afternoon at twelve I felt distinctly that death was approaching me from beneath; and thus I died from bottom to top, so that my whole body was so stiff that I felt nothing more of hands or feet, indeed nothing of my whole body; and finally I could not speak or see anything; for my mouth was so stiff that I could not open it up, and no longer felt it, and similarly my eyes; I could plainly feel them glazing over in my head. Nevertheless I understood the prayers that were being said at my bedside and heard one person say to another, "Feel how cold and stiff his legs are; he won't last much longer." I heard it, but did not feel it. When in the middle of the night the watchman called eleven, I heard it, but by midnight even my bodily hearing was gone.

Then it seemed to me that I was taken up with my whole body and swiftly led away, swifter than an arrow can leave the crossbow; and afterward, indeed, I inquired particularly whether my body had been away. But they told me that my body had not been away: As to how long my soul was away, this they could not truly make out. But I had been dead before their eyes, to the extent that my mother had already brought the shroud, and they were going to dress me in it: But God would not have it so, and blinded their eyes so that they could not notice that my soul was entranced out of the body, past the gates of hell and into heaven. It happened in an instant, for God can reveal and teach to a person in one moment more than one can utter in an entire lifetime. How this learning occurs, no man can grasp with his reason; it happened supernaturally in the spirit.

How long the soul was away, only God knows, no human. If my soul had remained in joy and splendor, my body would be lying in the churchyard long since. But in the middle of the night, when the watchman called eleven, the entrancement had not yet occurred; then I was stiff and cold and felt nothing of my body, nor could I see or speak; I had nothing left but bodily hearing. The people who were standing around me could not make out when my soul was at the gates of hell and in heaven. But when the watchman called twelve, the entrancement had already happened. Just as I had died from the bottom up, so I came back to life from the top down, till life had reached my feet again.

As I was being led back out of the clarity, it seemed to me as if

I were being laid down in place again with my whole body, and only then did I hear once again with bodily hearing that they were saying some prayers at my bedside. Thus hearing was the first thing I regained. After that I began to feel my eyes, so that my body regained its strength little by little. And when I felt my legs and feet again, I stood up again; and I was stronger than I had ever been in my life before: I was so strong from the heavenly joy that the people were very much startled that I became strong again so swiftly.

I am only a dead instrument, like a stiff organ pipe; when it is not being played on, it can make no sound. Know therefore that I too have been quite stiff and cold and could make no sound; that I now make sounds in speech is by the order of the Holy Spirit, and not by mine. I lay here lifeless as a glove; when there is no hand in the glove, the glove cannot move nor stir; but when a living hand thrusts itself inside, the glove can move. But the glove does not rule itself; rather the hand that has thrust itself into the glove moves in the glove and rules the glove; but the glove cannot rule itself. . . . So it is with me too. You have seen me lie here before your eyes like a dead glove that cannot move nor stir: but the living hand of God has thrust itself into me, into my dead flesh and blood when it was quite stiff and cold, and has made it live again through his heavenly power; and the almighty hand of God rules in me now, and not I.

HEMME HAYEN (second half of the seventeenth century)

FROM HIS LIFE STORY, TOLD BY HIMSELF AND FAITHFULLY WRITTEN DOWN BY HIS FRIENDS ON MAY 10, 1689

As the time of my enlightenment drew near, all our household were overwhelmed with outward afflictions. I often said to myself, "If God afflicts us, he is thinking of us." . . . But our house was visited with great sickness especially in the very week when God revealed to me the light of his mercy. . . . It happened that my son dislocated his foot. Therefore I sent on Saturday for a man of the Mennonites of Oldenborg, a village near Opgant, that he might examine my son's foot and that I might speak with him of his religion at the same time. But by Sunday morning, when he came to Opgant, God had already graciously visited me with his healing light. For on the morning of February 4, 1666, shortly before dawn, I was awakened by the power of this light, and my thoughts fell on certain sayings from Scripture, which I immediately understood in their spiritual meaning, and I had a very deep insight into them, such as had never occurred to me before. I thought of other words of Holy Scripture and immediately understood these too very clearly. Indeed, whatever came into my mind, I immediately understood in a spiritual way and had a supernatural, quite inexpressible and most highly superhuman heavenly sweetness and a communion with the universal being, so that I cried aloud with the excess of this joy and could not refrain from doing so.

Then I nudged my wife and said, as joyfully as I felt, "Child, are you awake?"

She was surprised that I spoke so joyfully and said, "Yes, I am awake, I hear you. What shall I do?"

I answered, "Now our dear Lord is giving me what I have prayed for so long."

At this she, like me, rejoiced not a little and was blissfully happy and said, "Ah, so now you have received it? That is good. But then why are you crying so?"

I answered, "I am crying for great joy." The whole time I cried out incessantly, and the joy was so unspeakably great that I could not refrain from crying.

When this had continued for some time, it gradually began to abate a little, so that I then stood up and put on my clothes, which I could not do before because of the great splendor of this grace. Meanwhile the Mennonite from Oldenborg arrived, looked at my son's leg, bandaged it, and because he had come at midday, ate with us. After the meal I went with him for part of his way home, and we got into a conversation on Jakob Böhme, for this enlightened man was very much in my thoughts. Then he said in a manner of speaking that is much in use among these people, "Was Jakob Böhme one of our people?" He meant one of his religion. This vexed and grieved me very much, that he wanted to bind the bliss of God to his congregation alone. Moreover, the light in me concealed itself during the time that we spoke together, but a certain glow remained.

When we had taken leave of each other I returned home and did not know whether anything more was still to come; but the inner work became so strong that I could not go out on the road for three days. During these days, especially on Monday and Tuesday, I was extremely restless. Now I sat for a while, now I walked to and fro in the house and was like a woman with child who is about to give birth. It was like a torment, and yet it must be called a sweetness more than a torment, for there was no vexation in it, but a strange, wholly supernatural pleasantness. At that time my body was inwardly so filled with it that I could distinctly feel the movement.

On Sunday evening I went to bed and slept the whole night. On Monday I rose early and kept myself free of all business. And when I was somewhat awake, I read in Isaiah from chapter 55 to chapter 61. Then I understood everything according to the inner ground and saw very clearly how the Spirit of God speaks there not only of the coming of Christ in the flesh, but especially of his coming according to the Spirit. For at that time I felt, as Paul says, that I no longer knew anyone according to the flesh. Indeed, whatever I read immediately became clear and shining in my heart, and I thought to myself, "How could I have been so blind before that I did not see this?" For some time after that I could no longer read, because the inner work was so great; I tried, but vainly. This grace became greater and greater the longer it lasted. It revealed itself especially strongly and with great power on Tuesday in a very pleasant taste, or rather in an inexpressible sweetness, such as nothing on earth can be. In the night from Monday to Tuesday and in the night from Tuesday to Wednesday I did not sleep at all, nor in the three nights that followed; and even in the night between Saturday and Sunday I slept scarcely at all. I did from time to time have a few soft sweetnesses and respites, but it could not be called sleep. The exalted working that was taking place in my spirit made it impossible for me to sleep.

But now I must continue telling what I left out. When on Wednesday morning the hardest work was over for this time, I went once more at eight or nine o'clock to Marienhofen, to visit the preacher Benjamin Potinius. But his brother, the preacher of Dornum, was with him and prevented me from speaking with him immediately, so that for a while I sat by their fire, though with vexation, for I wanted to speak to the preacher alone and tell him what had befallen me. Then it happened that the preacher's little son, a child of about three years, asked me for an apple, for he was used to my bringing him something when I came; but this time I had not thought of it, for my heart was too full. Then the father stood up and went into his study in order to bring an apple so that I might give it to the child.

I immediately followed right behind him into his study and said to him joyfully and eagerly, for I could not restrain myself, "Reverend preacher! Now our dear Lord is granting me the grace for which I have prayed to him for so long."

He said, "How so, Hemme Hayen?"

I said, "Because I now know and understand how a person can come to God and that it does not depend on the sect, but only on seeking God with one's whole heart. And as for the millennium—of which we spoke together not long since, when I was surprised that there were such opinions in Christendom, because I knew nothing—concerning this it has now become clear to me that there is a time which runs through the other time, with it and beneath it, but which is only felt and recognized by those to whom God gives grace. And now I have seen that there are many people who truly and authentically live this most blissful time."

When the preacher heard this, he was so moved that tears ran down his cheeks. I cried with him, indeed I was scarcely ever without crying, only when I forcibly restrained myself in front of people. We dried our tears and went back into the kitchen, where the other preacher was sitting by the fire. As it was midday, the preacher pressed me to eat with him, which I did. But from that day on I did not eat anything in the nine following days and nights, only sometimes took some drink for refreshment, for I was somewhat thirsty now and then. This seemed to me to mean the thirst for righteousness that was in me. Therefore I said to the people of my household, "May you people also thirst so for righteousness." But as for food, during that time it was too crude for me.

While we were sitting with the preacher at table, the two teachers spoke about various passages of Scripture. This seemed alien to me, and I said to myself, "How is this? It is quite otherwise with these matters, and they are so clear. How is it that they cannot understand?"

After the meal was finished I went home and constantly enjoyed a sweet communion with God. The next day, it was Thursday, it occurred to me to bring these joyful tidings to my sister too; she lived at Engerhofen, an hour south of Opgant. . . . When I came in she was sitting at the hearth with some work in her hands. The first thing I said to her was, "Sister, I am in heaven!" for the joy was so great that I burst forth and could not hold back. . . . We had a delightful talk, and toward evening I returned home, and my sister went with me for part of the way. Then I said to her, "There is yet a time ahead of me in which something strange will happen to me." But I myself did not know how, what, or when it should be or happen. I only felt it playing so in my heart and sometimes uttered the words before I thought. . . .

I went home, quite exalted with joy and inwardly brimful and glowing through and through, for I felt that I would faint with the splendor. For my body was too weak to bear this brightness. Then I pleaded, saying, "Lord, no more, or I shall burst!" And so in sweetness I reached home. At that time it reached its highest point, nor could it have been any higher because of the weakness of my body.

When I came home I found our people in bed and sat down myself in order to undress. Just then there was shown to me, sideward from the fireplace on a flat brick, a round thing, about the size of a rixdaler, all bright and clear with light like a crystal. At this my spirit rejoiced anew. But I wondered whether it was something particular or ordinary and went to the window to see whether it could be caused by the moon. But when I considered well I knew that the moon was not shining. I approached it once more and examined it with great wonder, and an inner voice said to me very distinctly, "That is a little piece of the new earth." After I had walked around it many times and had examined it sufficiently, it vanished again before my eyes.

See, this and the previous things awakened an ever-new astonishment in me. I considered the great things and contrasted my smallness with them. Then I went to bed. In one of these nights, I no longer know in which one, I received an altogether sweet sensitivity in the outward senses. Sight became so bright and hearing so lovely that the note I heard excelled all wordly melodies incomparably and proved sufficiently that it was heavenly. . . .

Everything was heavenly and quite perfect, so that it cannot be told to anyone as it happened. Only those who experience it once themselves or have experienced it can understand it.

The next day, Friday morning, as soon as day broke, I said to my wife, "Get up and make a great fire. For it is shown to me that today something wonderful will happen." I did not know just what; but that something was going to come, the Spirit had already announced to me. Thereupon my wife got up and made the fire. I also got up immediately, dressed and sat down by the fire. And immediately a dialogue began with me, as between a father and a son, which lasted about three hours, very clear and vocal, and I had to utter and answer everything with my natural tongue.

The members of my household, who were present, did not hear the speech of God, although it occurred in me very strongly and distinctly, and so I had to repeat it. This dialogue went on without the least deliberation in such a lively and merry way that it cannot be expressed, understood, or believed. Even the tone of voice was different for the father and for the son. The very beginning occurred softly and inwardly, without a voice, and afterward it became vocal. The son, that is, the new man who was born in me, said, "Father, do you play thus with your children? Are you so near to us? How could you have been so far away from us before?"

The father answered, "I have always been with you. Only what do you think of these things?"

I said, "Lord, you know. And I trust that this is you alone and that you alone are doing this, and no other."

The Nineteenth Century

ANNA KATHARINA EMMERICH (1774–1824)

The angel summons me and leads me hither and thither. I travel with him very often. He takes me to persons whom I do not know or have seen once; but also to such as are otherwise quite unknown to me. He even takes me across the sea; but that is swift as a thought, and then I see so far, so far! It was he who led me to the queen of France in her prison. When he comes to me to lead me on some journey, I usually see first a brightness, and then a form suddenly emerges shining from the night, as when the light of a dark lantern is suddenly uncovered. When we travel it is night above us; but a shimmer flies over the face of the earth. We travel from here through familiar landscapes to regions farther and farther away, and I have the sensation of uncommon distance. Sometimes we travel over straight roads; sometimes we cut across fields, mountains, rivers, and seas. I have to measure the whole way with my feet, and often even climb mountains with great effort. My knees are then painfully tired; my feet are burning; I am always barefoot.

My leader floats sometimes before me, sometimes beside me. I never see his feet move. He is very silent, without much movement, except that he accompanies his brief answers with a gesture of the hand or with a nod of the head. He is so transparent and shining, often very solemn, often mixed with love. His hair is smooth, flowing, and shimmering. He is without head covering and wears a long priestly robe with a blond shimmer.

I speak with him quite boldly, only I can never quite look him in the face, I am so bowed before him. He gives me every instruction. I avoid asking him many questions; the blessed contentment when I am with him prevents me. In his words he is always so short. I also see him while awake. When I pray for others, and he is not with me, I call him so that he may go to the other person's angel. And often when he is with me I say to him, "Now I'll stay here; you go there and bring consolation!" and I see him going that way. If I come to great waters and do not know how to get across, suddenly I am on the other side, gazing backward in astonishment.

I knew nothing of myself, I thought only of Jesus and my holy vows. My sister nuns did not understand me. I could not explain my state of mind to them. I was in the midst of it. But God had hidden from them many other mercies that he showed me, otherwise they would have been altogether misled concerning me. Despite all the pain and suffering, I was never so rich inside. I was overblissful. I had a chair without a seat and a chair without a back in my cell, and yet it was so full and splendid that all heaven often seemed to me to be within it. But when at night in my cell, enraptured by the love and compassion of the Lord, I sometimes burst into intoxicated familiar speech to him, as I have done since childhood, and someone must have been eavesdropping, I would be accused of great impudence and presumption toward God, and when once I could not help replying that it seemed to me a greater presumption to receive the body of the Lord without having spoken familiarly with him, oh, then I was much reviled.

With all this I lived with God and all his creatures in blessed peace. When I worked in the garden, the birds came to me, sat on my head and shoulders, and we sang praises to God together. I saw my guardian angel always at my side, and however much the foul fiend set others against me and even mistreated me himself with torture, beatings, and throwing, he could do me no great harm; I always had protection and help and forewarnings. My longing for the holy sacrament was so irresistible that I would often be drawn by it to leave my cell at night; in the church when it was open, or at the churchyard wall, even in the harshest winter, I would kneel or lie rigid with outspread arms, and thus the priest of the convent, coming early out of compassion in order to give me holy communion, would find me. When he approached and opened the church, I would awaken and hasten to the communion bench and find my Lord and God.

In my duties as sacristan my soul would often be as if suddenly snatched away, and I would clamber, climb, and stand in the church on high places—window frames, projections, and sculptures—which seemed humanly impossible to reach. Then I would clean and adorn everything. It always seemed to me that good spirits and beings were around me, holding me up there and helping me. I was not troubled about it; I had been used to it since childhood; I was never alone for long. We did everything together so pleasantly. Only among some people I was so alone that I could not help weeping, like a child that wants to go home.

I saw infinitely much that cannot be expressed at all. Who can say with the tongue what he sees otherwise than with the eyes? . . .

I see it not with the eyes, but it seems to me that I see it with the heart, about the middle of the breast. Sweat even breaks out there. At the same time I see through my eyes the objects and persons around me; but they do not know me, I do not know who or what they are. I am gazing now, even as I speak. . . . For several days I have been constantly between seeing with the senses and supernatural sight. I have to compel myself forcibly; for in the midst of conversation with others I suddenly see quite different things and images before me, and then I hear my own speech like that of another, and it sounds crude and muffled, as if the other were speaking through a barrel. I also feel as if I were intoxicated and might fall. My conversation with the speakers continues calmly and often in a more lively manner than usual, but afterward I do not know what I have spoken, and yet I speak quite coherently. It costs me considerable effort to maintain myself in this double state. I see what is present with my eyes, dimly, like someone who is falling asleep and already starting to dream. The second sight wants to snatch me away by force and is brighter than the natural sight; but it is not through the eyes.

Once when Anna Katharina had told a vision she put away her work and said: "I have been flying and seeing so the whole day that I sometimes see the pilgrim [Brentano]* and sometimes do not see him. Doesn't he hear the singing? I seem to be in a beautiful meadow, with trees arching over me. I hear such wondrously beautiful singing, like sweet children's voices. My close, real surroundings seem to me like a dream; everything around me seems so dull,

*Clemens Brentano (1778–1842), German romantic poet, from whose journal these confessions of Anna Katharina Emmerich are taken (editor's note).

opaque, and incoherent that it seems like a barbarous dream in whose intervals I see a light-filled world that is always understandable through and through, right through to the inner origin and coherency of all appearances; and in which what is good and holy delights more deeply because one recognizes one's way out of God and into God; and in which all that is evil and unholy grieves one more deeply because one recognizes one's way out of the devil and into the devil and against God and the creature.

"This life, in which nothing hinders one, not time, nor space, nor body, nor secrecy, where everything speaks and everything shines, seems so perfect and free that this blind, lame, stammering reality seems like an empty dream in it. In this prayer I became calm, and I saw a face approaching me, going into my breast, as if it were merging with me. And it seemed to me as if my soul in thus becoming one with the face shrank into itself and became smaller and smaller, and my body appeared to me as a crude, clumsy being, big as a house. The face, the apparition in me seemed as if threefold, became infinitely rich and manifold and yet was always one. It (that is, its rays, its looks) diffused into all the choirs of angels and saints. I felt consolation and joy over this and thought, 'Could all this be from the foul fiend?' And as I thought this, the images passed through my soul once more clearly and distinctly, like a procession of bright clouds, and I felt that they were now standing outside me in a bright circle. I also felt that I was larger again and my body no longer seemed to me so clumsy. It was only like a world outside me, into which I could gaze through an aperture of light. . . .

"The manner in which one receives communication from blessed spirits in a vision is difficult to tell. Everything that is said is uncommonly brief. From one word I learn more than otherwise from thirty. One sees the idea of the speaker, but one does not see with the eyes, and yet everything is clearer, more distinct than now. One receives it with pleasure, like the blowing of a cool breeze in hot summer. One can never repeat it wholly in words. . . .

"Everything this poor soul said to me was brief, as in all such communications, but the understanding has a greater difficulty with the speech of a soul in purgatory; its voice has something muffled, as if it sounded through a covering that dulled the tone, or as if someone were speaking from a well, or a barrel. At the same time the meaning is harder to grasp, and I must pay much closer attention than when my leader, or the Lord, or a saint speaks; for it is as if the words stream through one like a clear stream of air, and one sees and knows everything they say. One word puts more into our soul than a whole speech. . . . "

On July 25, 1821, Anna Katharina exclaimed to the pilgrim, "The pilgrim is without solemnity, and in fear he prays everything in confusion and very briefly. Often I see all sorts of evil thoughts running through his head; they look like the oddest nasty beasts! He does not catch them or drive them away quickly; it seems he is used to them. They run right through, as on a paved road."

The pilgrim observed concerning this, "That is very true, unfortunately!"

I see a line of words like a fiery ray come out of the mouth of those who are praying and penetrate up to God. I see and recognize in the words the handwriting of the one who is praying, and can read some of it. The writing is different with each person. In the stream itself some things become more flaming, some things more pale, now more expanded, now impetuous and more narrow. In short, it is just as with writing.

SUPPLEMENT

Ancient India

But now I will make known to you that blessed turning inward which brings about a hidden existence and which takes place in the middle of all beings by mild or harsh means.

That attitude for which virtue no longer counts as virtue, which is without attachment, solitary, and free from distinctions, which is completely dissolved in Brahman, is called the happiness that is directed to the sole place.

He who, as a wise man, draws desire from all directions back into himself as the turtle its limbs, such a man, passionless and free on all sides, is constantly happy; bringing back desires into his inner being, annihilating thirst, absorbed, benevolent and friendly toward all beings, he becomes fit for Brahmanhood.

Through suppression of all the sense organs that strive for things, and through avoidance of the dwelling places of men, the fire of his own self is united in the Muni [hermit, one who keeps silence].

As fire, fed with kindling wood, blazes up with a great brightness, so the great Atman [self] blazes up when the sense organs are suppressed.

When one contemplates all beings in one's heart with a calm self, then he serves as his own light, and from the hidden he arrives at the highest of all hidden things.

Its visibility is fire; what flows in it is water; its palpability is wind; its vile bearer of dirt is earth; and its audibility is ether; it is full of sickness and suffering, surrounded by the five river-gates [the five senses], woven together of the five elements, with nine entrances, inhabited by two gods [the highest and the individual soul], unclean, unsightly, constituted of the three gunas [qualities] and the three basic materials [mucus, gall, wind], addicted to touching and full of folly—that is the body, that is sure.

Difficult to handle everywhere in this world, having the intelligence as prop, the body rolls alone through this world on the chariot of time.

This terrible, unfathomable, vast ocean called delusion—one must put it aside, annihilate it, and bring the immortal world within one to its awakening.

Desire, anger, fear, greed, guile, and untruth, all these he throws off through subjection of the sense organs, although they are difficult to throw off.

Whoever while in the world has overcome these [organs] that are bound up with the three gunas and the five elements, his place is in heaven, and infinity becomes his portion.

The river which has the five senses for a great shore and the urge of Manas [here: the will] for a mighty current and which broadens out into the sea of delusion—one must swim through this river and overcome both, desire and anger.

Then, free of all frailties, one contemplates that highest thing, enclosing its Manas in one's own Manas and seeing the Self in one's own self. Omniscient in all beings, he finds the Self in himself by transforming himself into one or into many, now here, now there.

Then he sees through the forms completely, the way one ignites a hundred torches with one torch; then he is Vishnu and Mitra, Varuna, Agni, and Prajapati [the gods]; then he is creator and orderer, the Lord, the omnipresent, then he will radiate as the heart of all creatures, the great Atman; then hosts of Brahmans, gods, demons, demigods, monsters, shades and birds, flocks of goblins, throngs of ghosts, and all great wise men will sing his praise for evermore.

Chinese Mysticism

SAYINGS OF LAO-TSE AND HIS DISCIPLES

FROM THE BOOK OF WEN-TSE

He who penetrates the great universal harmony keeps himself withdrawn like one who is drunk from a noble wine and lies down with benevolent feelings. He moves in this immeasurable harmony as if he had never left the ground of the creation of beings. This is called the great penetration.

This is the action of the holy man. He moves toward the perfect void. He walks with his heart in the unconditional No. He strides out of all space. He takes his way where there is no door. He hears what has no sound. He sees what has no form. He does not cling to time. He has no fellowship with the uninitiated. Thus he moves the world.

FROM THE BOOKS OF TSCHUANG-TSE

The man who is like the spirits rises toward the light, and the barriers of the body are consumed. This is what we call sinking into the light. He raises the powers with which he is gifted to the utmost and does not leave a single quality unexhausted. His joy is that of heaven and earth. All things and all bonds pass away; all things return to their original nature. This we call enfolding oneself in the dark.

After three days the separation of things had ceased to exist for him.
After seven days the external had ceased to exist for him.
After nine days he stepped out of his own being.
After that his spirit became radiant as the morning, and he gazed on being, his I, face to face.
Having gazed, he became without past or present.
Finally he entered the kingdom where death and life are no more, and where one can kill life without making anything die and create life without making anything live.

Tse-khi of Nan-kuo sat leaning over his table. He looked up to heaven, breathed deeply and lightly and seemed remote, as if body and soul were separated. Yen Cheng Tse-yü, who stood before him, exclaimed, "What is this, that your body becomes like a withered tree and your spirit like dead ashes? Truly, the man who now leans over the table is not the same man who was here before."

Tse-khi said, "You are right to ask, Yen. I have buried myself today. Can you understand that? You may have heard the music of man, but not the music of earth. You may have heard the music of earth, but not the music of heaven."

FROM THE BOOK OF CONSTANT PURITY AND PEACE

He who can detach himself looks inwardly into his naked heart, and this heart is not his heart. He looks outwardly at his bodily form, and this form is not his form. Farther away he sees his objects, and these things are not his things.

FROM THE BOOK "THE RED-STRIPED CAVE"

I carry it uninterruptedly in my spirit: uninterruptedly penetrating, it abolishes all distinctions between life and death and makes me one with heaven and earth. When seeing is forgotten, the light becomes infinitely rich. When hearing is annihilated, the heart concentrates on the eternal depths. When the senses of perception are abolished, man becomes capable of unclasping himself from all charms of the world, purely, openly, and completely, in perfect union with the All; wide, limitless, like a vivifying breath of air, subject to none of the separations of humanity.

Jewish Mysticism

FROM THE HASIDIM

FROM THE HASIDIM, AN EASTERN JEWISH SECT ORIGINATING IN THE MID-EIGHTEENTH CENTURY

Fervor came over a tsaddik* each time the words "And God said" occurred in the reading of the Torah. A Hasidic sage who told this to his pupils added, "But I too think that when one speaks in truth and one receives in truth, one word is enough to lift up and purify the entire world."

In the earliest morning twilight a tsaddik stood at the window and, trembling, called out, "Just a short time ago it was still night, and now it is day—God is causing the day to arise!" And he was full of fear and trembling. Moreover he said, "Every created being should be ashamed before the Creator. For if he were perfect, as he was destined to be, he would have to be astonished and awaken and catch fire over the renewal of the creature at every time and in every moment."

It is told of one master that in times of entrancement he had to look at the clock in order to keep himself in this world; of another, that when he wanted to contemplate individual things he had to put on spectacles in order to subdue his spiritual sight, for otherwise he saw all the individual things of the world as one.

Once when a pupil noticed a tsaddik "growing cold" and found fault with this, he was informed by another, "There is a very high holiness. When one arrives there, one is freed from all nature and can no longer catch fire."

---

*Tsaddik: righteous man, holy man; name of the Hasidic rabbis, who are regarded as mediators between God and man (M. Buber).

Of a tsaddik's dancing it is told: His foot was as light as that of a four-year-old child. And all who saw his holy dancing—there was not one who did not return home to himself, for it inspired in the hearts of those who saw it both weeping and bliss in one.

A tsaddik stood in prayer during the "Days of Awe" (New Year and Day of Atonement) and sang new melodies, wonder of wonders, which he had never heard and which no human ear had ever heard, and he had no idea what he was singing or what melodies he was singing, for he was bound to the higher world.

It is said of one master that he conducted himself like a stranger, according to the words of King David: "I am a stranger in the land." Like a man who has come from a foreign country, from the city of his birth. He does not think of honor or of anything for his own benefit. He thinks only of returning home to the city of his birth. Nothing can possess him, for he knows, "That is alien, and I must go home."

On his deathbed a tsaddik asked his grandson, "Do you see anything?" The grandson looked at him in astonishment. "I," said the tsaddik, "no longer see anything but the divine nothingness, which gives life to the world."

Sayings of the Hasidim

When a man has fulfilled the whole Torah and all the commandments but has not had the bliss and the ardor, when he dies and crosses over, they open paradise for him, but because he did not feel bliss in the world, he does not feel the bliss of paradise.

A man should learn pride and not be proud, should know anger and not get angry. Man can mortify himself with all blisses. He can look toward whatever place he likes, yet not lose himself beyond his four cubits;* he can listen to jesting words and be heavy-hearted. And so it happens that he sits here and his heart is above, he eats and drinks and pleasures himself in this world and enjoys from the world of spiritual blessedness.

_____

*In the Talmud four cubits denotes minimal personal space (editor's note).

A man can speak idle words with his mouth, and the teaching of the Lord is in his inner being at the same time; he can pray in whispers, and his heart cries out in his breast; he can sit in the company of men, and walk with God, mingling with the creatures, yet detached from the world.

Whoever greatly desires a woman and contemplates her brightly colored garments has his mind not on the gorgeous cloth or colors, but on the splendor of the desired woman who is enveloped in them. But the others see only the garments and nothing more. So whoever desires and receives God in truth beholds in all the things of the world only the power and the pride of him who shaped them at the primal beginning, and who lives in things. But whoever is not on this level sees things as separate from God.

When it is granted to man to hear the songs of the herbs—how every herb speaks its song to God without any alien will or thought —how beautiful and sweet it is to hear their singing. And therefore it is very good to serve God in their midst in solitary walks over the field among the plants of the earth and to pour out one's speech before God in truthfulness. All the speech of the field then goes into your speech and heightens its power. With every breath you drink the air of paradise, and when you return home, the world is renewed in your sight.

As the hand held before the eye covers the greatest mountain, so this little earthly life conceals from sight the tremendous lights and secrets of which the world is full. And whoever can remove this life from before his eyes, the way one removes a hand, sees the great shining of the world's inwardness.

Occasionally one may experience the separation that there are so many other firmaments and spheres, and he stands on one point of the little earth, and the whole world is as nothing before God, who is the limitless one and who made limitation and set location in himself in order to make the worlds. And although he grasps this with his understanding, he cannot climb up to the upper worlds, and so it seems to him as if he were seeing God from a distance. But if he serves with his might, then he clings to the great might and elevates himself in his mind and breaks all at once through all the firmaments and transcends angels and hypostases and seraphim and thrones: That is the perfect service.

The creation of heaven and earth is the unfolding of something out of nothing, the descent of the higher into the lower. But the saints, who detach themselves from being and cling to God constantly, see and grasp him in truth, as if the nothingness were as it was before the creation. They turn something back into nothing. And this is the more wonderful thing: to uplift what is below. As it is written in the Gemara, "Greater is the last wonder than the first."

Ecclesiastical and Nonecclesiastical Mysticism of the Early Christian Period

FROM THE WRITINGS OF MAKARIOS THE EGYPTIAN (301–391)

When the soul clings to the Lord, and the Lord, moved by compassion and love, comes to the soul and clings to it, and the mind remains constantly in the grace of the Lord, then the soul and its Lord become one spirit, one nature, and one mind. And while the body of this soul lies on earth, its spirit lives wholly in the heavenly Jerusalem, rises to the third heaven, attaches itself to the Lord, and serves him. And he who sits upon the throne of glory and exaltation in the heavenly city is entirely with the soul in its body. For he has established the image of the soul in the holy city of the saints, in the higher Jerusalem; but his own image, the image of his secret light and his divinity, he has established in the soul's body. He serves the soul in the city of the body, while the soul serves him in the heavenly city. The soul possesses him as its inheritance in the heavens, and he, on the other hand, possesses the soul as his inheritance on earth. For the Lord becomes the inheritance of the soul, and the soul becomes the inheritance of the Lord.

FROM THE WRITINGS ASCRIBED TO DIONYSIUS THE AREOPAGITE

FROM THE COMPOSITION ON MYSTICAL THEOLOGY

Therefore Saint Bartholomew says that divine wisdom is manifold and at the same time small; the Gospel is wide and great and at the same time condensed. It seems to me that he means this supernaturally: that the cause of all things is at once rich in words, laconic, and wordless; that it possesses neither speech nor thought, since it lies superessentially over all that is and appears in its unveiled truth only to those who transcend all guilt and innocence and all ascent to holy heights, and who leave all divine lights and sounds and plunge into the darkness where, as Scripture says, he truly is who is beyond everything.

And not for nothing was the divine Moses commanded first to purify himself, then to separate himself from those not purified, and after all the purification he hears the trumpets of many notes and sees many lights that cast pure and manifold beams; then he separates himself from the throng and, with the elect priests, comes to the height of the divine ascent. After all this, however, he is still not associated with God; he does not see the Invisible, but only the space upon which he stands. . . . But then he is freed even from what is seen and from the seer and plunges into the darkness of unknowing, the truly mystical darkness in which he casts off all contradictions of knowledge and is received into what is altogether impossible to grasp or to contemplate; he now belongs entirely to the one who is beyond all and who belongs to nobody, neither to himself nor to another; through the abolition of all knowing he is united in the core of his being with the completely unknowable, and in knowing nothing, he knows beyond the spirit.

From the Tract "Sister Katrei"

ASCRIBED TO MEISTER ECKHART

Now the aforementioned daughter comes again to her confessor and says, "My lord, hear me, for God's sake." He said, "Where do you come from?" She said, "From distant lands." He said, "Who are you?" She said, "Do you not recognize me?" He said, "God knows I do not." She said, "That is a sign to me that you have never known yourself." He said, "That is true. I know that if I knew myself as I should—that is, most closely—I would know all creatures." She said, "That is true. Now let us leave this talk. Hear me for God's sake." He said, "Gladly; say what you have to say." The daughter makes her confession to her reverend confessor as it is in her to do, so that his soul rejoices within him. He says, "Dear daughter, come to me soon again." She says, "If God so wills, I shall be glad to."

He goes to his brothers and says, "I have heard a human being speak and do not know whether it is a human being or an angel. If a human being, then know that all the faculties of her soul dwell with the angels in heaven, for her soul has received an angelic nature. She knows and loves beyond all human beings of whom I have ever had knowledge." The brothers say, "God be praised."

The confessor seeks the daughter in the church where he knows she is and begs her sincerely to speak with him. She said, "Do you not know me yet?" He said, "No, God knows." She said, "Then I will tell it to you out of love. I am the poor creature whom you drew to God." Then she reveals to him who she is. He says, "Ah, poor man that I am, how I must be ashamed before God's eyes that I have borne the appearance of spirituality for so long and have discovered as yet so little of God's mystery." He says, "I beg you, dear daughter, for the love you bear God, that you reveal to me your life and the exercises you have practiced since I last saw you." She said, "Of this there would be much to tell." He said, "It cannot be too much; I hear it gladly. Know that many wonderful things have been told me of you." The daughter begins and says to her confessor, "You must never betray me, as long as I live." He says, "I give you my promise that I will never betray your confession as long as you live." She begins and tells him so many wonderful things that he is struck with wonder that a human being can suffer so much. She said, "My lord, I still lack something; I have gone through all that my soul desires, except the one thing, that I have not been accused because of my faith." He said, "Praised be God that ever he created you; now let it content you." She said, "Never, as long as my soul has no constant dwelling at the place of eternity." He said, "It would content me if my soul had the constant ascent that yours has." She said, "My soul has a constant ascent without any obstacle; but it does not have a constant dwelling. Know that time is not enough for me; if I only knew what I must do to be confirmed in constant eternity." He said, "Have you such great desire of this?" She said, "Yes." He said, "You must be bare of that desire, if you are ever to be confirmed." She said, "I do it gladly," and places herself in bareness. Then God draws her into a divine light, so that she imagines that she is one with God, and so she is, as long as this lasts.

Then the divine feeling bounds back, and she is thrown back into herself, so that she says, "I do not know if there is any help for me." The confessor goes to the daughter and says, "Tell me, how fare you now?" She said, "Ill; heaven and earth are too narrow for me." He asks her to tell him something. She said, "I know nothing so clear that I could tell it." He said, "Do it for God's sake; tell me a word." Then she speaks to him so wonderfully and deeply of the naked sensation of divine truth that he said, "Know that that is alien to all humans, and if I were not a learned priest, so that I have learned it myself in theosophy, it would be unknown to me too." She said, "I begrudge you that; I would that you had found it with your life." He said, "You should know that I have found so much of it that I know it as well as that I read mass today. But know that it is a grief to me that I have not yet taken possession of it with my life." The daughter says, "Pray to God for me, and go back into your solitude and enjoy God." But it is not long before she again comes to the door and asks for her reverend confessor and says, "My lord, rejoice with me, I have become God." He says, "God be praised. Now go back into your solitude, away from all people; if you remain God, I am glad for you."

She obeys her confessor and goes into a corner of the church. Then she went so far that she forgot everything that ever acquired a name and was drawn so far out of herself and all created things that she had to be carried out of the church and lay till the third day, and they thought she was certainly dead. The confessor said: "I do not believe that she is dead." Know that, had it not been for the confessor, she would have been buried. They tried every means of determining whether the soul was still in the body, but could not find out. They said: "Certainly she is dead." The confessor said: "Certainly she is not dead."

On the third day the daughter comes to herself again and says, "Alas, poor me, am I here again?" The confessor comes to her immediately and says to her, "Let me enjoy divine faithfulness; reveal to me what you have experienced." She said: "God knows I cannot. What I have experienced, no one can put into words." He said: "Have you now all you desire?" She said: "Yes, I am confirmed."

She said: "I had concentrated all the faculties of my soul. When I looked into myself, I saw God in myself and everything God ever created in heaven and on earth. I will relate this to you still better. You know that whoever has entered into God and into the mirror of truth sees everything that is judged according to that mirror, that is, all things. This was my inner exercise before I was confirmed. Have you understood the meaning?" He said: "It must needs be true. Is your present exercise, then, not of such kind?" She said: "No. I have nothing to do with angels or saints or anything that was ever created. More: I have nothing to do with anything that has ever become word." He said: "Instruct me better." She said: "I am doing so. I am confirmed in naked divinity, in which never image nor form existed." He said: "Are you constant in this?" She said: "Yes." He said: "Know that this speech I am glad to hear, dear daughter; speak on." She said: "Where I stand no creature can arrive in a creaturely manner." He said: "Instruct me better." She said: "I am where I was before I was created; where there is only bare God in God. In that place there are no angels or saints or choirs or heaven. Many people tell of eight heavens and nine choirs; where I am that is not. You should know that all that is put into words and presented to people with images is nothing but a stimulus to God. Know that in God there is nothing but God. Know that no soul can enter into God unless it first becomes God just as it was before it was created.

"You should know, that whoever contents himself with what can be put into words—God is a word, the kingdom of heaven is also a word—whoever does not want to go further with the faculties of the soul, with knowledge and love, than ever became word, ought rightfully to be called an unbeliever. What can be put into words is grasped with the lower senses or faculties of the soul, but the higher faculties of the soul are not content with this; they press on, further and further, until they come before the source from which the soul flowed. But you should know that no faculty of the soul is able to enter the source. The nine faculties of the soul are all slaves of the soul's might, and they help that might to come before the source, drawing it forth from the lower things. When the soul stands in its majesty before the source, above all created things, the might of the soul penetrates into the source, and all the faculties of the soul remain outside.

"You must understand this thus: The soul is naked and bare of all things that bear names. So it stands, as one, in the One, so that it has a progression in naked divinity, like the oil on a cloth, which spreads and keeps on spreading and spreading until it has flowed over the whole cloth. So you should know that as long as the good person lives in time, his soul has a constant progression in eternity. That is why good people cherish life."

Bibliography

The following editions and translations were used for this work:

BABA LAL H. Wilson: *Sketch of the religious sects of the Hindus.* Calcutta 1846 (also published earlier in Asiatic Researches XVII).

RAMAKRISHNA Max Müller: *Râmakrishna. His life and sayings.* London and Bombay 1898. Swami Vivekananda: Speeches and writings. Madras 1905. *The sayings of Sri Ramakrishna Paramahamsa.* Madras 1905. *Gospel of Sri Ramakrishna.* I. Madras 1907.

RABI'A A. Tholuck: *Ssufismus sive theosophia Persarum pantheistica.* Berlin 1821. Ibn Challikan: *Biographical dictionary,* translated by de Slane. I. Paris 1842. Tezkereh-i-Evlia. *Le mémorial des saints,* traduit par A. Pavet de Courteille. Paris 1889.

HUSSEIN AL HALLADJ A. Tholuck: *Blütenlese aus der morgenländischen Mystik.* Berlin 1825. Cf. Louis Massignon, *Kitâb al Tawâsîn,* Paris 1913; see also his essay in the *Revue de l'histoire des religions* 1911 and that of H. Lammens in the *Recherches de science religieuse* 1914.

BAYEZID BISTAMI *Tezkereh-i-Evliâ. Le mémorial des saints,* trad vit par A. Pavet de Courteille. Paris 1889. A. Tholuck: *Ssufismus sive theologia Persarum pantheistica.* Berlin 1821. For the beginning of the next-to-last passage, where the wording of the translation seemed questionable to me, I was able to compare the Persian text through the kindness of Professor Dr. Gotthold Weil.

FERID-ED-DIN ATTAR *Mantic Uttaïr ou le langage des oiseaux,* traduit par Garcin de Tassy. Paris 1863. *Pend-Namèh ou le livre des conseils,* traduit par Silvestre de Sacy. Paris 1819. (In his notes de Sacy has translated passages from the "Conference of the Birds" from another text than that used by Garcin de Tassy.)

JALAL-ED-DIN RUMI *Masnavi i ma'navi,* translated by E. H. Whinfield. London 1887. Selected poems from the *Divâni Shamsi Tabrîz,* translated by R. A. Nicholson. Cambridge 1898.

THE DISCIPLES OF MOLLA-SHAH A. de Kremer: *Molla-Shah et le spiritualisme oriental.* Paris 1869.

PLOTINUS IV. Enn. 8,1; VI. Enn. 9,9,11. (Plotini, *Enneades,* ed. H. F. Mueller, Berlin 1878).

VALENTINUS *Hippolytus Phil.* VI. 42, V.37. Cf. H. Weinel: *Die Wirkungen des Geistes und der Geister im nachapostolischen Zeitalter.* Freiburg i. B. 1899.

MONTANISTS The words which have been preserved are collected in N. Bonwetsch, *Die Geschichte des Montanismus,* Erlangen 1881.

SYMEON Του δσιου χαι θεοφορου πατρος ήμων Συμεων του νεου ξεολογου τα ε'ρισχομενα. Venice 1790. Συμεων του νεου θεολογου τα ε'ρισχομενα παντα in *Mignes Patrologiae Graecae* T. CXX. Paris 1864. For individual passages I have used the Munich manuscript for textual comparison.

HILDEGARD *Analecta Sanctae Hildegardis opera Spicilegio Solemensi parata,* ed. J. B. Card. Pitra. Paris 1882. (The letter is addressed to Guibert of Gembloux.)

ALPAIS *Vie de la bienheureuse Alpais, publiée pour la première fois en latin d'après un manuscrit chartrain du XIII. siècle par l'abbé P. Blanchon.* Marly-le-Roy 1893.

AEGIDIUS *Chronica XXIV Generalium Ordinis Minorum* (Analecta Franciscana III). Quaracchi 1897. The legend concerning King Louis is given according to the text of the *Actus beati Francisci et sociorum ejus* (ed. Sabatier, Paris 1902), which is older than that of the Fioretti.

MECHTILD VON MAGDEBURG *Offenbarungen der Schwester Mechthild von Magdeburg,* herausgegeben von P. Gall Morel. Regensburg 1869.

MECHTILD VON HACKBORN *Revelationes Gertrudianae ac Mechtildianae* II. Paris 1877.

GERTRUD *Revelationes Gertrudianae ac Mechtildianae* I. Paris 1877.

SEUSE Heinrich Seuse: *Deutsche Schriften,* herausgegeben von Karl Bihlmeyer. Stuttgart 1907.

CHRISTINA G. W. K. Lochner: *Leben und Gesichte der Christina Ebnerin, Klosterfrau zu Engelthal.* Nürnberg 1872. P. Strauch: *Margaretha Ebner und Heinrich von Nördlingen.* Freiburg i. B. and Tübingen 1882. Two passages are taken from the Stuttgart manuscript. See also Strauch's communications in the *Anzeiger für deutsches Altertum* IX.

MARGARETA P. Strauch: *Margaretha Ebner und Heinrich von Nördlingen.* Freiburg i.B. and Tübingen 1882.

ADELHEID *Die Offenbarungen der Adelheid Langmann, Klosterfrau zu Engelthal,* herausgegeben von Philipp Strauch. Strassburg 1878.

THE ADELHAUSEN CONVENT J. König: *Die Chronik der Anna von Munzingen.* (*Freiburger Diöcesan-Archiv* XIII. Band. Freiburg i.B. 1880.)

THE TÖSS CONVENT *Das Leben der Schwestern zu Töss,* beschrieben von Elsbet Stagel, herausgegeben von Ferdinand Vetter. Berlin 1906. The Nürnberg manuscript was consulted. Other documents of German monastic ecstasy in: *Der Nonne von Engelthal Büchlein von der genaden überlast.* Tübingen 1871. Bernhard Pez, *Biblioteca ascetica* (Regensburg 1723/6) VIII. (See also Catharina von Gebsweiler: *Lebensbeschreibungen der ersten Schwestern der Dominikanerinnen zu Unterlinden,* deutsch von T. Clarus 1863.) *Chronik des Bickenklosters zu Villingen* (by Juliana Ernst), hsg. v. K. J. Glatz. Tübingen 1881. *Leben der Schwestern zu Diesenhofen,* hsg. v. Anton Birlinger, *Alemannia* XV. (1870). Other material in *Alemannia* XI. and XXI. (Kirchberg) and the *Zürcher Taschenbuch* for 1889 (Oetenbach).

THE SONG OF BARENESS Tauler: *Von eym waren Evangelischen Leben.*

Köln 1543. The last stanza, which returns to a dogmatic view and seems as if artificially attached, has been omitted.

BIRGITTA *Revelationes caelestes sanctae matris Birgittae.* Munich 1680.

JULIANA *Revelations of divine love shewed to Mother Juliana of Norwich.* London 1902. (Title of first edition: *XVI Revelations of Divine Love, Shewed to a Devout Servant of our Lord, called Mother Juliana, an Anchorete of Norwich.* 1670.)

GERLACH PETERS *Gerlaci Petri Soliloquia Divina.* Paris 1659.

ANGELA *Beatae Angelae Fulginatis vita et opuscula.* Foligno 1724.

CATHERINE OF SIENA *Raimondo da Capua: La vita di Santa Caterina da Siena.* Milan 1842.

CATHERINE OF GENOA *Marabotto e Vernazza: Vita mirabile et dottrina celeste di Santa Caterina Fiesca Adorna da Genova.* Padua 1743.

MARIA MADDALENA *Vita e ratti di santa Maria Maddalena de' Pazzi.* Lucca 1716. Puccini: *La vita di santa Maria Maddalena de' Pazzi vergine nobile Fiorentina.* Venice 1675.

TERESA *Cartas de Santa Teresa de Jesus.* I.II. Madrid 1771 and 1778.

ANNA GARCIAS From her autobiography (German translation: Cologne 1669), reprinted in Tersteegen: *Auserlesene Lebensbeschreibungen heiliger Seelen.* II. Frankfurt and Leipzig 1735.

ARMELLE NICOLAS *L'ecole du pur amour de Dieu ouverte aux savans et aux ignorans dans la vie merveilleuse d'une pauvre fille idiote païsanne de naissance et servante de condition.* Nouvelle édition. Cologne 1704. German: *Die Schule der reinen Liebe Gottes.* Augsburg 1736.

ANTOINETTE BOURIGNON *La vie de Dlle. Antoinette Bourignon.* (Oeuvres I.) Amsterdam 1683.

JEANNE MARIE GUYON *La vie de Madame J.M.B. de la Mothe-Guyon,* écrite par elle-même. Nouvelle édition. Paris 1791.

CAMISARDS *Theatre sacré des Cevennes.* London 1707. (Cf. also Elie Marion: *Avertissements prophétiques* 1707.)

BÖHME *Morgenröte im Aufgang.* Amsterdam 1682.

THE PAGE Stephanus Praetorius: *58 schöne, auserlesene geist- und trostreiche Traktätlein von der güldenen Zeit.* Goslar 1622.

ENGELBRECHT *Der vom Tode erweckte Protestant, oder des Einfältigen Busspredigers Hans Engelbrechts Schriften.* 1761.

HEMME HAYEN *Levensloop van Hemme Hayen.* Haarlem 1714. German version in J. H. Reitz: *Historie der Wiedergeborenen.* 4. Aufl. V. Bd. Itzstein 1717. Another translation appeared under the title: *Lebensgeschichte des Hemme Hayen, eines niederländischen Bauern und wahrhaften Clairvoyanten.* Nürnberg 1810.

KATHARINA EMMERICH The diaries of Clemens Brentano, from which the text is taken, have not yet been published in their entirety. Some of the passages I have quoted are found in K. H. Schmöger: *Das Leben der gottseligen Anna Katharina Emmerich* (2. Aufl. Freiburg i.B. 1873), others in *Das bittere Leiden unsers Herrn Jesu Christi. Nach den Betrachtungen der Anna Katharina Emmerich,* which has seen many editions. Cf. also K. Emmerich: *Das Leben Jesu Christi*, Regensburg 1858–60, and idem., *Leben der heiligen Jungfrau Maria* (many editions).

FROM THE MAHABHARATAM The translation has been taken from Paul Deussen's book, *Vier philosophische Texte des Mahabharatam*. Leipzig 1906.

LAO-TSE F. H. Balfour: *Taoist texts, ethical, political and speculative*. Shanghai 1884. J. Legge: *The texts of Tâoism* (The sacred books of the East. XXXIX. XL). Oxford 1891. C. de Harlez: *Textes tâoï'stes* (Annales du musée Guimet. XX). Paris 1891. H. A. Giles: *Chuang Tzu, moralist, mystic and social reformer*. London 1899. Buber: *Reden und Gleichnisse des Tschuang-Tse*. 5. Aufl. Leipzig 1922. The main work of the school, Lao-tse's *Tao-te-king*, exists in several translations, among which those of Alexander Ular (Leipzig 1903), Viktor v. Strauss (Leipzig 1870; this translation approaches a faithful understanding of many passages more closely than Ular's linguistically daring version), and Richard Wilhelm (Jena 1911) are noteworthy.

THE HASIDIM Buber: *Die Geschichten des Rabbi Nachman*. Frankfurt a.M. 1906. Buber: *Die Legende des Baalschem*. Frankfurt a.M. 1908. Buber: *Der grosse Maggid und seine Nachfolge*. Frankfurt a.M. 1921. The next-to-last passage is taken from a still-unpublished translation.

MAKARIOS SS. PP. Gregorii Thaumaturgi, *Macarii Aegyptii et Basilii Seleuciae opera omnia*. Paris 1622.

DIONYSIUS Migne: *Patrologiae Graecae* T. III. IV.

KATREI I have used text of the St. Gallen manuscript, and have also consulted the Anton Birlinger ("Traktate Meister Eckharts," *Alemannia* II, 1875) and the Franz Pfeiffer manuscript (*Deutsche Mystiker des 14. Jahrhunderts* II, Leipzig 1845) for purposes of comparison. For information on the state of textual criticism see Otto Simon: *Überlieferung und Handschriftenverhältnis des Traktates Schwester Katrei*. Halle a.S. 1906.

For further literature the following references must suffice:

ON THE SUFIS: E. G. Browne, *A Literary History of Persia* I, London 1902 (in which, however, only hostile sources on al Hallaj are used); I. Goldziher, *Vorlesungen über den Islam*, Heidelberg 1910; R. A. Nicholson, *The Mystics of Islam*, London 1914; R. A. Nicholson,* *Studies in Islamic Mysticism*, Cambridge 1921; A. V. Kremer, *Geschichte der herrschenden Ideen des Islam*, Leipzig 1868; Adalbert Merx, *Grundlinien einer allgemeinen Geschichte der Mystik*, Heidelberg 1893.

ON SYMEON: Karl Holl, *Enthusiasmus und Bussgewalt im griechischen Mönchtum*, Leipzig 1898, and his article in Herzog-Hauck, *Realenzyklopädie*, 3. Aufl., Bd. XIX.

The Mystics of Islam, London 1914; R. A. Nicholson,